101

Grade A

Résumés

for Teachers

Second Edition

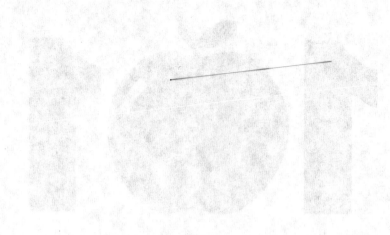

101

Grade A

Résumés

for Teachers

Second Edition

by Rebecca Anthony and Gerald Roe

BARRON'S

ABOUT THE AUTHORS

Rebecca Jespersen Anthony and Gerald Roe are career specialists at The University of Iowa. They have written numerous articles on employment and the job search, with an emphasis on academic careers. Authors of seven books, including *The Curriculum Vitae Handbook* and *Over 40 and Looking for Work,* they have developed specialized training packets for career professionals and have co-directed national studies dealing with employment and hiring issues in education.

The authors have served in leadership positions in professional associations and are frequent presenters at conferences and seminars.

DEDICATED TO

Tas, Natalya, Tassie, Veronica,

Steve, April, Dave,

Anthony, Allison

Always, with kind thoughts of Maggie,
Peabody, and Clara in Wyoming who give us
inspiration and a laugh or two.

All inquiries should be addressed to:
Barron's Educational Series, Inc.
250 Wireless Boulevard
Hauppauge, New York 11788

Library of Congress Catalog Card No.: 97-29628

International Standard Book No. 0-7641-0129-3

Library of Congress Cataloging-in-Publication Data
Anthony, Rebecca, 1950–
    101 Grade A résumés for teachers / by Rebecca
Anthony and Gerald Roe.—2nd ed.
      p.   cm.
      On title page the 0 in 101 is represented by an "apple."
      ISBN 0-7641-0129-3
      1. Teachers—Employment. 2. Résumés
(Employment) 3. Cover letters. I. Roe, Gerald.
LB1780.A677 1998
808'.06665—dc21
                                      97-29628
                                      CIP

PRINTED IN THE UNITED STATES OF AMERICA
987654321

CONTENTS

PREFACE

There is no shortage of books about résumés. Any good bookstore can provide several books about résumé preparation, with countless samples of résumés in a variety of formats. Recent additions to the literature include advice about designing digitized résumés to be posted on the Internet or crammed with key words that will attract the attention of an impartial and inanimate electronic scanner.

When teachers look into these books, they do not find themselves reflected there, although in sheer numbers—not to mention the significance of what they do—teachers comprise a substantial portion of the workforce. According to the National Center for Education Statistics, there are 2.7 million teachers in public schools today. Private schools employ more than 404,000 teachers. And, because these figures represent full-time equivalents, thousands more individuals must be counted as professional educators. Teachers deserve a book about résumé preparation that is designed expressly for them.

An educator's résumé is only superficially like résumés in the business sector. Not only is the vocabulary of a teacher's résumé different from other occupations, even within the profession there is considerable variation from state to state and from region to region. Similarly, a teacher's achievement is not measured in quite the same way. Teachers and school administrators cannot rely on numbers to document efficiency or to prove productivity. Promotion is not an issue for the classroom teacher, and profitability cannot and must not be the bottom line.

The first edition of this book grew out of more than twenty years of work with thousands of new and experienced teachers. Response to that edition indicates that beginners and veteran educators have found the book of genuine help in promoting their various skills and qualifications to potential employers. We believe that educators at every level can find themselves reflected in these updated and expanded pages.

PART ONE

YOUR
RESUME

1
WHAT IS A RESUME?

A résumé is a summary of experience. That's all it is, just a summary of experience. It is not a technical blueprint, an autobiography, a testament, or an essay. A résumé is not a legal document, nor is it a formal declaration prepared according to standard specifications. Computer generated or typewritten, printed or electronically stored and retrieved, a résumé is a summary of experience—period.

Myths and mysteries have grown up around the subject, making many people, particularly those who are preparing to write their first résumé, think they face a task of great difficulty. Consequently, they procrastinate, they copy the first model they see, or they try to find someone to prepare a résumé for them.

WHO KNOWS YOU BEST?

The truth is, *you* are the expert. You are the person best qualified to put yourself on paper. Considering the importance of a résumé in today's marketplace, you would be foolish to allow anyone else to do it for you. No one can do it better.

Even if you are just beginning your career in education, you have found many occasions to create a paper profile. You filled out applications to be admitted to college and more forms to enter a teacher preparation program. You know how to provide information to the Internal Revenue Service, a bank, a financial aid office, a credit card company. You could almost consider yourself an expert at filling out forms.

Unfortunately, you may never escape the struggle to fit the shape of your life into a form of someone else's devising. But preparing a résumé is less complicated and far more interesting than merely filling out forms. In the first place, *you* get to decide what's most important. You decide what you want to highlight; you even decide what you'd just as soon not call to anyone's attention. You control the presentation, you design the format, and you create your best professional image.

FITTING INTO PRESCRIPTIVE MODELS

All of the information you will use to build your résumé could be forced to fit neatly or awkwardly into various prescribed models. Traditionally, two principal types of résumé have been touted and promoted: chronological and functional. Lengthy discussions of their differences, and their inherent advantages and disadvantages, have been carried on among career development professionals in books and articles and more recently in electronic bulletin boards and news groups.

Briefly, a chronological résumé takes a historical approach. The résumé focuses on dates and locations, listing educational background and work record, including job titles and names of employers. A functional résumé, on the other hand, emphasizes competencies, abilities, and achievements without necessarily relating them to a specific work experience or time frame.

Too often, strict adherence to either model will limit an educator's ability to make the most advantageous presentation. Each model has features that can capture the reader's attention and promote specific strengths. The most effective features of chronological and functional approaches can be combined in a résumé that emphasizes your unique personal and professional attributes.

The proliferation of personal computers and rapid advances in electronic communication have made résumé preparation both easier and more complicated. Access to a personal computer and a letter-quality printer are all that is required to create an effective résumé. Prepackaged software-driven prescriptive models are widely available and easily accessed. For some job seekers, packaged programs are entirely adequate and can save time, but you need to question whether the program offers sufficient flexibility to present special skills and abilities. Will the program allow you to project your best image, your most marketable skills or experiences?

No single prescribed model should dictate the format, arrangement, or organization of your résumé. Common sense, combined with your particular priorities, should be the hallmark of your presentation.

2
EDUCATORS NEED RESUMES

Like professionals in many other fields—marketing, finance, engineering, medicine, science, government, and social service—educators need to know how to prepare and use a résumé. But different professions require different approaches, different treatments, different vocabularies. A résumé must be particularly suited to the profession as well as to the individual. A model résumé for a marketing director will be of no help to a third grade teacher.

A marketing résumé must reflect a business image. Accomplishments and potential should be described in terms of increased sales, reduced expenses, improved productivity, time saved, and advancement from one position to another. Stating accomplishments in terms of dollars and cents, percentages, increases and decreases, and profits and losses is reasonable and effective.

A teacher's résumé, however, only superficially resembles the typical business model. The focus, the emphasis, the vocabulary, and the overall message are different. Teachers should not attempt to follow the dictates of other occupations. The result will not strike the appropriate tone, nor will it focus on educational objectives. Teachers do not have a product, educational progress is not always and not necessarily measured in percentages, promotion is hardly an issue, and profitability is not the bottom line.

KNOW YOUR CULTURE

Caution: Each profession has its own culture, its own way of doing things, and to some extent its own language—certainly its own jargon. Do not use the language or techniques of another occupation to seek a teaching position. It is all too easy to adopt catchy terms and fashionable phrases, but educators must take care to stay within their own culture. Inappropriate use of popular buzz words can signal a lack of understanding of the profession or a misguided attempt to appear more knowledgeable or more qualified.

Even within the field of education, terminology is not uniform. Because each state has the responsibility of providing a system of public instruction for its citizens, the vocabulary and the definition of conditions, programs, and services is not uniform throughout the country.

The terminology used in a particular state to describe a teaching specialization may be quite different from terms used even in neighboring states. Each state approves educational programs for its schools, determines requirements for certification, and issues licenses for teachers and administrators.

The problem is compounded by abbreviations and acronyms referring to teacher preparation programs, modes of instruction, and organizational systems. Although you may be familiar with several of these common abbreviations, you cannot assume that your reader will understand what is meant by IEP, CLP, BD, ELD, ED, LD, ESL, TOEFL, MR, MMMI, MH, BH, ADD, ADHD, AEA, CESA. Instead of using abbreviations, it is a good idea to spell out the terms, especially if you send your résumé to employers in other states.

SELF-PROMOTION IS GOOD PRACTICE

All successful job seekers have marketing plans. Teachers, too, must learn how to promote themselves, how to sell their skills and abilities to employers. Your challenge is to create a professionally appropriate résumé; a résumé that reflects your culture and that promotes you as a committed educator with experiences and abilities that are—if not unique—clearly consistent with current practices and procedures.

The first résumé you write will most likely be used in a job search. As your career develops, you will find many other occasions to prepare and submit a résumé. A résumé is an essential document for every educator at every stage of a career.

A good résumé is an indispensable marketing tool for:

- student teachers

- first-year teachers

- experienced teachers

And for:

- substitute teachers

- paraprofessionals

And for:

- supervisors

- consultants

- principals

- superintendents

Whether you are a novice or a veteran, if you are or if you want to become one of these educators, you need a résumé.

3

WHAT GOES INTO A RESUME?

A résumé is built on facts: facts about you, your education, your background, your experiences. A good résumé presents the facts in a logical and meaningful sequence, telling potential employers who you are and what you have done, capturing their interest, and leading them to the desired conclusion.

Forcing the reader to solve a puzzle or unravel a mystery story deprives you of the opportunity to make a good first impression. You rarely have the luxury of a second chance.

THREE ESSENTIALS

Start with the basics. Be sure to include clear and direct information about these three essential items:

1. Identity

    Use your legal name, your full address, and your telephone number. Zip codes and area codes are important. So are FAX numbers and E-mail addresses. This information seems obvious, but personnel departments and hiring officials frequently receive résumés lacking an address or other contact information.

2. Educational Background

    List academic degrees earned or in progress, major or field of study in which degrees were earned, and dates conferred or expected. Accuracy and honesty are critical.

3. Teaching Experience

    Any teaching experience (including full- or part-time professional experience, student teaching, practica, and internships) can be included on a résumé. Substantial professional experience can make it unnecessary to list early training experiences.

COMPILING RESUME FACTS

Take a few minutes to fill in the blanks with facts about yourself. Once you have listed these basics, you will have all the material you need to begin working on a draft of your résumé.

Identification

Name _____

Records under other names _____

Address _____

Telephone _____

FAX Number _____

E-mail Address _____

URL Internet Address _____

It may be necessary to list both a temporary and a permanent address. It is permissible to indicate a termination date for the temporary address: for example, until June 1.

Education

Degree-granting institutions: _____

Institution and Location _____

Attended from: _____ to:

Degree earned or in progress _____

Graduation date _____

Major: _____ Minor:

Area(s) of specialization: _____

Institution and Location _____

_____

Attended from: _____ to:

Degree earned or in progress _____

Graduation date _____

Major: _____ Minor:

Area(s) of specialization: _____

_____

Other institutions attended: _____

Institution and Location _____

Attended from: _____ to:

Major: _____ Minor:

Area(s) of specialization: _____

_____

Institution and Location _____

Attended from: _____ to: _____

Major: _____ Minor: _____

Area(s) of specialization: _____

_____

Teaching Experience

Information about internship experience or student teaching is essential for beginners and optional for teachers with professional experience. After more than a year or two of professional experience, information about preprofessional experience is generally included only if it indicates a different area of expertise or a significantly different grade level.

Position: _____

Employer: _____

Name and location of school or organization

Dates of Employment: _____ to: _____

Accomplishments: _____

_____

_____

Position: _____

Employer _____

Name and location of school or organization

Dates of Employment: _____ to: _____

Accomplishments: _____

_____

_____

BUT I HAVEN'T DONE ANYTHING SPECIAL...

Once you have completed the three basic sections, you might wonder what other information you need to incorporate. Procrastination can easily set in if you are convinced that you don't have anything but the basics to put into a résumé. Don't take this shortsighted view. You have a multitude of possibilities for additional sections. All teachers, beginners and experienced alike, have many special achievements, accomplishments, and significant experiences to relate.

Yes, everyone else completed student teaching or an internship. But no one had your particular experience. No one else achieved the same things, taught the same units, developed your unique style of teaching, or motivated the students in quite the same way. Very few people have taken exactly the same course work as you or had identical job or volunteer experiences.

It is a mistake to assume that your experiences are ordinary. Any hiring official will assume you have spent some time in a classroom in order to earn a teaching license. But no assumptions can be made about your achievements, your successes, your singular approach to good teaching. It is up to you to let your strengths be known.

A Special Note: Be careful not to overlook any unusual educational experiences. Special programs, summer institutes, foreign study tours, or a semester or year abroad can capture an employer's attention and make your resume stand out from the others in the pile. Most employers realize that educators who seek these supplemental experiences tend to be independent, intellectually curious, and committed to learning.

WHAT, NOT WHEN

Don't be unduly influenced by dates. What you have done is certainly more important than when you did it. For example, honors or other special recognitions rarely lose their impact. If you were inducted into Phi Beta Kappa twenty years ago, you can still consider this distinction a relevant item for your résumé. Being selected student body president, outstanding history student, or receiving the Volunteer of the Year award retains value long after the recognition was bestowed.

MORE FACTS...

In order to assemble additional facts for your résumé, the following checklist can help you recall previous experiences and activities. Quickly read through the list and check as many *Yes* responses as you can. Then come back and jot down the specifics. Don't worry about when it happened or the level of importance at this point. Don't worry about vocabulary and phrasing, either; just record the basic information. When you're ready to write a rough draft of your résumé, you can develop full-fledged entries based on your responses. Assigning priorities, refining the language, and polishing the individual sections will come later.

Yes No

❑ ❑ Language abilities

_____

_____

❑ ❑ Technology Skills

_____

_____

☑ ❑ Study or travel abroad

_____*Ireland*_____

_____

Yes No

❏ ❏ Professional memberships/elected offices

_____

_____

❏ ❏ Leadership positions (campus/community)

_____

_____

☑ ❏ Conference attendance/participation

_____ NCCTM _____

_____

☑ ❏ Volunteer activities/civic contributions

____ Secret Pal Programs _____

_____

❏ ❏ Professional recognition

_____

_____

❏ ❏ Honors, awards, distinctions

_____

_____

❏ ❏ College activities

_____

_____

❏ ❏ Avocations and interests

_____ Travel, Computers _____

_____

❏ ❏ Community service/service learning

_____

_____

❏ ❏ Exhibits, shows, publications

_____

_____

Yes No

❏ ❏ Grants, special projects

_____

_____

❏ ❏ Teaching competencies

_____

_____

❏ ❏ Extracurricular interests

_____

_____

❏ ❏ Professional development

_____

_____

❏ ❏ Recent courses of interest

_____

_____

❏ ❏ GPA (overall & major)

_____

_____

❏ ❏ Other work

_____

_____

❏ ❏ Other

_____

_____

DO I NEED A JOB OBJECTIVE?

In some occupations, a job objective is both traditional and useful; consequently, many people consider a job objective indispensable and expect to see it right at the top of the résumé. As an educator, however, you can convey a professional objective in a number of ways. You can express your interests, preferences, or priorities as _Teaching Competencies_, _Teaching Interests_, or _Special Skills_. Training in multiple teaching techniques, strategies, or methods and exposure to different teaching styles or settings can be communicated to a potential employer at a glance. Other sections of your résumé reinforce your objective and contribute to convincing the reader of your competence or expertise.

A useful job objective is clear, specific, and unencumbered with extraneous words. If you include an explicit statement of your job objective, restrict it to the nature of the position:

> Head basketball coach
>
> Journalism teacher and student newspaper advisor
>
> Bilingual kindergarten teacher

A note of caution: Too often, objectives look like this:

> Objective: To obtain a position that is challenging, rewarding, and affords opportunity for personal growth and professional development.

Examine that statement. What does it say? And what message does it send? A close look reveals a mere series of words and phrases that are correct and proper and good and safe but have no real significance. They sound prefabricated if not pretentious. This calculated objective is too general to be of any use and is simply a waste of your space and the reader's time.

EVALUATING AND SELECTING

Look at all the things you have listed and select those entries that contribute to the image or picture you want to present to potential employers. Not everything is of equal value or importance, and you may decide that some items are no longer relevant and do not justify using space that could be taken by more current or more pertinent information.

Carefully and thoughtfully select items that emphasize your strongest assets and greatest interests.

ARRANGING YOUR INFORMATION

As you look over your list of facts and previous experiences, you will see that some of them can naturally be grouped together. Your résumé can have several sections representing different aspects of your educational background, interests, and experience. Each section can be assigned a descriptive heading to attract and to direct the reader's attention.

As you organize your material, the following list can help you select appropriate headings for the sections or divisions of your résumé.

SUGGESTED HEADINGS FOR YOUR RESUME

Degree(s)	Study Abroad
Educational Background	Course Highlights
Education	Courses of Interest
Educational Preparation	Academic Highlights
Academic Training	Course Concentration

Teaching Certificate(s)

Certificate(s)

License(s)

Licensure

Endorsements

Coaching Certification

Other Certification

Career Objective

Teaching Objective

Job Objective

Objective

Professional Objective

Position Desired

Teaching Strengths

Skills and Competencies

Teaching Competencies

Teaching Skills

Areas of Expertise

Areas of Knowledge

Special Skills

Special Talent

Computer Training

Multimedia Expertise

Technology Skills

Teaching Experience

Professional Experience

Classroom Experience

Teaching Overview

Experience Highlights

Related Experiences

Student Teaching

Internship Experience

Practicum Experience

Practica

Field Experiences

Professional Seminars

Workshops Attended

Special Training

In-service Training

Professional Activities

Current Activities

Exhibits

Shows

Performances

Publications

Presentations

Conference Participation

Seminar Presentations

Language Competencies

Language Ability

Languages

Travel Abroad

Travel

Overseas Travel

Foreign Experiences

International Experiences

Overseas Study

Professional Leadership

Professional Memberships

Affiliations

Professional Societies

Honorary Societies

College Distinctions

College Activities

Special Recognition

Academic Honors

Achievements

Honors and Distinctions

Awards

Scholarships

Extracurricular Interests

Coaching Skills

Coaching Interests

Club Advisor

Class Sponsor

Service

Committee Responsibilities

Committee Assignments

Departmental Service

Civic Contributions

Community Service

Community Activities

Civic Activities

Community Involvement

Volunteer Activities

Activities

Leisure Activities

Avocations

Interests

Employment

Other Work

Part-time Work

Summer Work Experience

Additional Experience

Nonteaching Experience

Military Service

Other Experiences

References

Credentials

Credential File

Placement File

BREAKING THE ONE-PAGE RULE

Teachers often need more than one page to present a complete account of their qualifications, especially if they have professional experience in the classroom. Depending on the number of field-based experiences, even a beginner may find it necessary to use more than a single page.

By contrast, people in the business world usually try to restrict a résumé to a single page. A new graduate in finance or accounting would consider a second page unconventional and likely to create an unfavorable impression. Even a person with considerable experience might hesitate to expand to a second page. So powerful is the mystique surrounding a single-page résumé that even people who should not be bound by this rule are afraid to abandon it.

Quantity alone, however, is not the goal. There is such a thing as padding: Overzealous descriptions, annotations that pile detail upon insignificant detail, or long tedious lists of the most minute or routine activities can have the effect of trivializing every aspect of the résumé. Fit all relevant information on a single page if you can, but do not be afraid of offending the reader by expanding your resume beyond this arbitrary limit.

The goal of a résumé is to stimulate interest, not to overwhelm with detail. A résumé should be as long as it needs to be and as short as it can be.

Employers in education are more inclined to focus on the content than on the length. And they will be more favorably impressed with a résumé that is easy to read and pleasing to the eye.

4
WHAT GETS LEFT OUT?

Contrary to what you may have heard, it is not necessary to list every activity, include details of every experience, or account for every year. Your résumé is not your permanent record, your autobiography or a blueprint for your future.

Ambitions, dreams, speculations, long-range plans, and ultimate goals have their place in a job search. But they don't belong on your résumé.

BE CONSISTENT

Your résumé must agree with all information provided to an employer, but it does not have to duplicate other documents or contain every bit of data on your educational background. Employers will ask for your transcript, which will list all courses taken as well as grades earned and degrees conferred. Grade point average is not a standard entry on a teacher's résumé.

In the initial screening process, most hiring officials are not overly concerned with your grade point average. They scan your résumé to find evidence of your educational qualifications, your teaching experiences, and your demonstrated interest in working with children or youth. Unlike some employers in the business sector, school officials do not restrict serious consideration to candidates with a predetermined grade point average. Good grades are always an asset, never a detriment. But scholastic achievement is valued in combination with other special skills you can offer in the classroom. A high GPA does not guarantee that you will work successfully with children.

If your educational record gives the impression that you were a peripatetic student roving from campus to campus, you might want to list on your résumé only the institution that granted your degree. This is not a technique to deceive employers but a way to save valuable space to promote your teaching abilities. You are not obligated to list on your résumé every institution you have attended. The school district's application form will likely request a complete educational record, and your official transcripts will show attendance at all institutions from which you have transferred credits.

WHAT ABOUT REFERENCES?

The initial screening process usually does not require names and addresses of individual references and you need not waste space or time in providing them. Application forms almost always ask for references; there is no advantage to duplicating this information or providing names and addresses before they are requested.

If a job announcement specifically asks for names and addresses of references, you may choose to list them at the end of your résumé, make a separate reference listing page, or include their names and contact information in your application letter. Always get permission to list a person as a reference.

Give a copy of your current résumé to each person who has agreed to serve as a reference for you. The résumé will help your recommender to provide accurate information regarding your experiences and abilities.

CUTTING OUT THE DEADWOOD

Experienced professionals should carefully review information about preprofessional training. Retaining outdated information can increase the length but not the impact of your résumé. Lists of practica or student teaching experiences that occurred several years ago are seldom worth the space they occupy. Moreover, they can divert attention from recent and more important professional development.

Activities dating back to high school or even college years may have little relevance to your current objective and are probably best omitted. There are always exceptions to this rule, however. For example, if you are qualified and interested in promoting yourself as a basketball coach but did not play on a college team, you could reach back to high school and briefly mention your participation in team sports. If you were an all-conference player or selected to an all-state team, the information will add some credibility to your potential as a coach. Similar examples could be given for yearbook sponsorship, cheerleading, debate, or any other school activity. If you are seeking a teaching position at a preparatory school or a parochial institution, it is probably a good idea to mention that you attended a similar school.

Your résumé is not an official document; you have the opportunity and the responsibility to determine the facts you want to present and the skills you want to emphasize.

DON'T WRITE YOUR AUTOBIOGRAPHY

During the selection process, all information requested by an employer should be job related. Hiring officials should not solicit information about marital or family status, disabilities, age, gender, race, ethnic background, religion, height, weight, or color of eyes and hair. Obviously, this personal data is not job related. Because it does not affect your qualifications or your potential as an educator, there is no reason for you to volunteer this kind of information.

Providing unsolicited personal data to employers may be a detriment to yourself and to the employer. Federal and state guidelines prohibit employers from getting preemployment information of this sort. Applicants who supply this type of information actually place a burden on the employers who must devise procedures to discount potentially discriminatory information.

DON'T BELIEVE EVERYTHING YOU SEE...OR HEAR

Old books on library or resource center shelves (even some shiny new books at your local bookstore) contain examples and advice that should have been discarded years ago. These are the samples that helped your father or your Uncle Jack to land a job. In a prominent place, usually on page one immediately after the name and address, they listed information about their age, height, weight, marital status, wife's name if appropriate, and at least the number of children if not their names and ages. If the spouse or child had accomplished something significant, that might be included, too.

Because this type of résumé worked for them, Dad and Uncle Jack will probably advise you to put in the same sort of personal information. They may even suggest that you include a photograph of yourself, as they did, either by attaching a photo or actually having it printed on the page.

- Do not listen to them.

- Times are different now.

- Laws have been enacted to prevent discrimination.

- Including personal information is unsophisticated and reflects outmoded practices.

- And never—ever—unless you are seeking work as a model or performer—send a photograph.

DON'T CLUTTER YOUR RESUME WITH NONESSENTIALS

Space on your résumé is valuable. Include only those items that can help you to promote your skills and abilities to potential employers. Don't squander space on irrelevant information. The employer will see it as a waste of time and interpret it as your inability to organize thoughts and data.

Your résumé does not need and should not contain these items:

1. *Title.* Reserve the most prominent location for your name. The reader will recognize a résumé without seeing the word "RESUME" as the first line of the first page. Keep the focus on you; a label is distracting and unnecessary.

2. *Philosophy Statement.* Your beliefs about teaching and the process of learning will very likely enter into the selec-

tion process, but do not use résumé space for this purpose. A statement of your personal educational philosophy may be requested as a part of the application form or as a question during an interview.

3. *Personal Statement.* Your résumé is not the proper vehicle for conveying biographical details about your upbringing or your early educational experiences. Similarly, how you chose to pursue a teaching career, how you propose to conduct your classroom, or what you see yourself doing in the future are excellent topics for responses to open-ended questions on the application form or during the interview.

4. *Reason for Leaving Previous Position.* In a business résumé, it is sometimes considered possible to make a positive statement of professional growth by citing reasons for leaving a position. One can show a progression, indicate greater opportunity for responsibility or higher earnings, or promotion to a new project or level. This practice does not work for teachers, and there is no reason to attempt to define your career path in business terms. Educators work in a different environment and a different culture, and they define their achievements with a different vocabulary. They can change positions, change responsibilities, and change job titles, but the system does not allow for promotion.

5. *Availability.* There is no need to state that you will be available for a position beginning immediately or at a specified future date. Hiring officials will assume that you can begin when needed. Although emergencies or unforeseen circumstances can require immediate hiring, starting dates are not usually open to negotiation. The selection process is geared to the academic year or to the beginning of a semester or trimester.

6. *Date Prepared.* Your résumé will be considered current so long as it reflects your latest experiences. Assigning a date, however, can make it appear outdated within a few months even though nothing has changed. Let your cover letter serve to indicate the date your résumé was submitted.

7. *Ability to Travel or Relocate.* This is another carryover from the business world with little application to the field of education. Teachers might divide their responsibilities between schools in the same district, but overnight travel is simply not a factor for classroom teachers. A teacher may transfer from one building to another within a district, but because school districts are local entities,

such transfer would rarely require changing one's residence.

8. *Salary.* Public school teachers generally do not have the opportunity to engage in individual negotiation for salary or benefits. A master contract governs placement on the salary scale, number of working days, holiday schedules, and conditions of employment. Salaries vary from district to district, from state to state, and from region to region. Whether your previous salary exceeds or falls short of the possibilities in the district to which you are applying is of no consequence; therefore, salary history has no place on your résumé.

NO APOLOGIES, NO EXCUSES

If you have gaps in your education or in your employment record, a history of job-hopping, even if you have been fired, you can stress the positive aspects of your experience. Pay special attention to how you organize this material. For example, if you have frequently moved from job to job, you won't want to emphasize dates of employment. They can be placed at the end of the entry, or even buried in the middle. You are not being deceptive; you are emphasizing the experience rather than the chronology.

If health problems caused an interruption in your career, the gap might be apparent to a careful reader, but you should not attempt to explain it. Any illness serious enough to cause a job interruption tends to frighten prospective employers. Save your explanation for the interview when you have the opportunity to demonstrate that you are physically capable of discharging your duties and responsibilities.

Because you control the material presented in your résumé, you have the opportunity to present yourself in the best possible light. This does not mean you can be less than truthful. Every item on the résumé should work to your advantage: Stress the positives, avoid ambiguous or questionable entries, and weed out any item that could be construed as a negative. Accuracy and honesty are paramount, and misrepresentations, exaggerations, or actual lies are never acceptable.

As you begin to design your résumé, refer to the following model to remind you of what goes in and what gets left out.

ADDRESS: (Include city, state, zip, phone, E-mail, URL Internet address.)

RELEVANT EXPERIENCE: (List place, date, and brief description about field experiences, internships, practica, teaching assistantships, and student teaching experiences.)

RELATED ACTIVITIES: (Expand on projects or teaching-related activities, volunteer service, and community contributions.)

EMPLOYMENT: (List title of position, employer, location, and dates; briefly describe duties if related to teaching objective.)

ACTIVITIES AND DISTINCTIONS: (Include leadership positions, academic honors, and professional associations.)

EDUCATION: (State degrees held or in progress, certificates, licenses.)

INTERESTS: (Include academic, athletics, avocations.)

REFERENCES: (Indicate placement office or state that references available upon request.)

WHEN YOU PREPARE YOUR RESUME, REMEMBER–

- **NO** picture
- **NO** personal information (age, sex, race, marital status)
- **NO** information about children, spouse, or significant other
- **NO** physical data (eye or hair color, weight, height)

5
ACTIVATE YOUR RESUME

The ability to write cohesive paragraphs employing a balanced variety of simple, complex, and compound sentences is a decided asset. This skill, however, is not required in writing a résumé. You can appropriately demonstrate your mastery of the language in your application letter and in other writing samples you may be asked to submit. At some point in the selection process, you will almost inevitably be asked to produce a short essay (often handwritten) describing your philosophy of education or your reasons for wanting to work in the district. Your résumé requires a different style of communication.

Active.

Quick.

Concise.

Convincing.

Action words and dynamic phrases create powerful impressions. Energize your activities, your skills, your accomplishments, with strong active language.

BE SELECTIVE

Avoid repetition; the impact of any word is diminished by too frequent use. Let's say you have developed five new instructional units that demonstrate your interest in several different curriculum areas. Your first draft might read like this:

Developed geography unit for third grade

Developed multigrade unit on the solar system

Developed...

Obviously, this leads to monotony. Almost any approach would be better. An easy way to retain the impact of several similar activities without constant repetition might be:

Developed instructional units for various grade levels, including:

Looking at Latitude and Longitude (Grade 4)

Our Solar System (Grades 3–4)

Fractions are Fun (Grade 4)

Alphabets and Hieroglyphics (Grade 3)

Proper Nouns and Proper Caps (Grade 3)

USE ACTION WORDS

The following list of action words should help you get started. You can use some of these, or find other powerful verbs to create a dynamic picture of you and to suggest your potential.

Accomplish	Collect	Discover
Achieve	Commended	Distinguish
Acquired	Communicate	Distribute
Act	Compete	Diversify
Adapt	Compile	Draft
Address	Complete	Edit
Administer	Compose	Educate
Advance	Compute	Eliminate
Advise	Conceptualize	Enable
Analyze	Conduct	Encounter
Approve	Conserve	Encourage
Arbitrate	Consolidate	Enlist
Articulate	Consult	Establish
Assemble	Contribute	Evaluate
Assess	Control	Examine
Assist	Coordinate	Execute
Attain	Correspond	Expand
Author	Counsel	Explain
Balance	Create	Facilitate
Budget	Critique	Familiarize
Build	Deliver	Find
Catalog	Design	Focus
Chair	Develop	Formulate
Clarify	Devise	Generate
Coach	Diagnose	Group
Collaborate	Direct	Guide

Identify	Organize	Revise
Illustrate	Originate	Revitalize
Implement ✓	Overhaul	Rewarded
Improve	Oversee	Schedule
Incorporate	Participate	Screen
Increase	Perform	Select
Influence	Plan	Serve
Inform	Prepare	Shape
Initiate	Present	Skilled
Innovate	Preside	Solidify
Install	Process	Solve
Institute	Produce	Sponsor
Integrate	Program	Stimulate
Interpret	Project	Streamline
Interview	Promote	Strengthen
Introduce	Provide	Study
Invent	Publicize	Summarize
Investigate	Publish	Supervise
Involve	Received	Survey
Launch	Recommend	Systematize
Lead	Record	Teach
Lecture	Recruit	Test
Maintain	Reduce	Train
Manage	Refer ✓	Translate
Mediate	Rehabilitate	Travel
Moderate	Repair	Trim
Monitor	Replaced	Upgrade
Motivate	Represent	Utilize ✓
Network	Research	Validate
Nominated	Restore	Venture
Observe	Restructure	Verify
Obtain	Reverse	Work
Operate	Review	Write

Action words must be used accurately. Find a way to describe your role in any activity that neither overstates your case nor undervalues your achievement. If you chaired a committee, say so; just listing the name or function of the committee ignores your leadership role. On the other hand, if you were a member of a team that developed a new learning center, be careful about claiming all of the credit.

Discrepancies have a way of surfacing. Avoid placing yourself in a potentially awkward or embarrassing position.

SHORT PHRASES = EASY READING

One of the most effective methods of giving energy and life to your résumé is to make the writing flow easily and quickly. Complete sentences, however well constructed, cannot be read as quickly as fragments. Short phrases with strong verbs are easy to scan, conveying your message clearly and dynamically without verbal excess, redundant auxiliary verbs, or a clutter of personal pronouns. How long can anyone sustain interest when each sentence begins:

I was

I did

I have

I am

I made

I...

You get the idea. Sentence fragments allow you to skip over the repetitive personal pronoun and get directly to the important part, the activity or accomplishment, and to lead off each entry with a strong verb.

Suppose you found this on a résumé:

I have had the responsibility in April of each year for putting together the Washington School talent show which earned money for the general fund.

Look at the difference when an action phrase replaces a complete sentence:

Created and organized profitable annual school talent show

By combining your activities with strong action verbs, the phrases on your résumé might look something like this:

- Utilized effective classroom management strategies

- Planned, prepared, and organized materials for thematic units

- Provided consistent enthusiasm and creativity in classroom activities

- Individualized instruction for students at all levels and abilities

- Facilitated the implementation of writing and reading strategies in ten elementary buildings

- Developed a training packet for portfolio assessment

- Instituted a new curriculum that included long-range plans to incorporate computer literacy into daily instruction

Action words and phrases in your résumé will produce a significant bonus. When you begin to interview for positions, you will already have the habit of expressing yourself in language that makes you sound vital, energetic, and enthusiastic.

CREATE YOUR OWN ACTION PHRASES

On the lines below, write action phrases that describe your skills, abilities, and accomplishments.

_____

_____

_____

_____

_____

_____

_____

_____

_____

CONSIDER PRIORITIES

As you incorporate these phrases into your résumé, try to match the significance of the item to its place on the page. Generally, you will want to lead with your strengths. The most important item should appear first.

PRODUCTION GUIDELINES

Nothing about your résumé is more important than what it says about you, but potential employers may not pay attention to the content if the appearance does not create a good first impression. Imagine reading twenty résumés—or fifty, a hundred, a thousand, or more. Many hiring officials face exactly this task when they need to hire a teacher.

What can you do to make their job easier?

A hiring official responsible for reviewing application materials must look for quickly identifiable reasons to reject at least a portion of the applicants. Judging a résumé by its appearance requires comparatively little time or effort, and it is a standard and legitimate practice.

The old adage about not judging a book by its cover does not apply here. An unprofessional appearance makes a résumé easy to discard.

RESUME LAYOUT

The arrangement of material on the page is referred to as the layout. The position and alignment of the information in the various sections of your résumé can make a vital difference in how you are perceived. Don't rush this stage of your résumé development. The samples in this book use several different layouts. Experiment with the effect of different layouts on your material. An effective layout guides the reader through the information about your education and experience, directing attention to your strengths while allowing the reader to assess your résumé easily and quickly.

Although there are no prescribed layouts for résumés, three styles are commonly used because they are easily prepared and professional in appearance.

Layout #1
This résumé is set up with a full block style. Every heading begins at the left margin, creating a sharp, clean look. Locations, dates, and other details about professional background are uniformly indented from the left. The shorter line necessitated by this style makes it especially appropriate if you have a limited amount of material.

J. J. TOPHER

221 College Street, Any City, State 12345 (101) 555-0009
jjtopher@ ubrown.edu

TEACHING SKILLS

Japanese, grades 6-12
English as a Second Language, all levels

DEGREES

M.A. Asian Studies, Brown University, Providence, 1999
    Japanese with Teaching Certification Program
B.A. Major: Linguistics; Minor: East Asian Languages, 1997

INTERNSHIP

Japanese, grades 6-12, Bellton Academy, Providence, Fall 1999
- Taught Japanese on 4 levels including a newly created Honors Class
- Assisted in the coordination of interdisciplinary projects with social studies classes and art classrooms
- Integrated technology into daily teaching with specialized software, video discs, CD-ROMs, and WWW research
- Developed alternative assessment methods including portfolios

ESL EXPERIENCE

English Teacher, Osaka Schools, Osaka, Japan, 1997-1998
- Team-taught, with Japanese mentor, English in three high schools
- Created daily lesson plans on grammar, spelling, and vocabulary
- Developed numerous supplementary teaching materials to use in the classroom and to share with students for nightly review
- Presented seminars and workshops to area teachers and participated in several cultural exchange programs

AFFILIATIONS

Rhode Island Second Language Educators
Association of Teachers of Japanese

PART-TIME WORK

Interpreter, Wong Travel Agency, Providence, 1998-present
Tutor, Japanese language, private students, 1998-present
Web page designer, Rhode Island Design Solutions, 1998

REFERENCES

Available upon request.
Visit my Web site at www.topher/esl.htm

Layout #2

This résumé uses centered section headings, and full margins for each entry. The wider line readily accommodates a larger volume of information. With appropriate indentation to allow for ample white space, the résumé can handle a longer text without resorting to dense blocks of print. It can also handle a shorter text if several indentations are made within entries or additional space separates each section.

COO E. LIGHTFOOT

221 College Street   Any City, State 12345   (101) 555-0009

OBJECTIVE

Teacher: Multiage, Multilevel Elementary Education (K-8)

SPECIAL SKILLS AND INTERESTS

Collaborative Planning	Cooperative Learning
Proactive Classroom Management	Team Teaching
Community Service Emphasis	Individualized Learning
Thematic Approach to Lesson Design	Inclusion
Multicultural Awareness and Teaching Style	Technology Integration

ACADEMIC BACKGROUND

Bachelor of Arts Degree, *with honors* University of North Carolina-Chapel Hill, December 1999

Major: Elementary Education; Area of Specialization: English/Language Arts and Technology

COURSE HIGHLIGHTS

Manual Communication	Literature for Children	Creative Drama in Classroom
Microcomputers for Teachers	Linguistics	Classroom Management
Adolescent Literature	Exceptional Learner	Computer Programming

STUDENT TEACHING EXPERIENCE

Multilevel grades, West Middle School, Big Horn District 121, Horizon, Idaho, Fall Semester 1999
Work in a collaborative setting with a team of six multilevel teachers in a rural school with 175 students of varied abilities, ages 4 to 13 years. Responsibilities include initiating, planning, and implementing service learning projects; integrating reading and writing, grammar, phonics, and spelling into a holistic and individualized curriculum; coordinating and teaching math lessons and activities; observing all subject areas and various teaching techniques; organization of homeroom and beginning-of-day activities for all students; planning, preparing, and organizing materials for thematic units used by various age groups; enhancing and increasing the use of computer technology in the class; and introducing student-led conferences and facilitating student portfolio development.

PRACTICA EXPERIENCE

3rd grade, all subjects including math, science, spelling and language arts, Elk Elementary, Fall 1999
4th-6th grade, community service project-environment and pollution, Hills Elementary, Summer 1999
Multiage, multimedia (computer basics, Internet, CD-ROMs, videodisc) Elk Elementary, Fall 1998
1st grade, reading tutor for at-risk students using integrated approach, Hills Elementary, Spring 1998

References available upon request.

Layout #3

This résumé style positions the section headings at the left margin, allowing a wide line for entries. Because the entire page can be used, it is a good choice if you need to include extensive descriptions or a number of different experiences. To use space effectively, the address is spread across the page directly below the name. A corresponding horizontal line at the bottom of the page gives it a finished appearance.

BRAD EMILIA

221 College Street, Any City, State 12345 (101) 555-0009
brad-emilia@sfsuniv.edu   www.brad/bay.htm

TEACHING INTERESTS AND STRENGTHS

Alternative High School Instructor
 Academic strengths in English, History, Math, and Psychology
 Student-Centered Approach with Emphasis on Goal-Setting
 Strong Collaborative Skills

INTERNSHIP EXPERIENCE

San Francisco East Alternative Center, September 1999 to December 1999
 - Worked in a diverse urban school alternative setting that fostered enthusiasm
   for learning by encouraging student participation and creativity.
 - Involved students in goal-setting, course and career planning.
 - Used innovative methods and materials to produce effective learning experiences
   that built student pride and increased self-worth.
 - Developed, with mentor teachers, new course syllabi and materials in Fine Arts.
 - Encouraged students to take responsibility for own learning experiences.

PRACTICA EXPERIENCE

At-Risk and Community Liaison, S.E. Junior High School, Oakland, Spring 1999
 - Counseled and worked closely with students who are failing or have extensive
   absences due to home situations, jobs, or poor study habits and lack of basic skills.
 - Communicate with parents/guardians, parole officers, and social agencies regularly.
 - Maintain careful records and document activities and academic progress.

DEGREES

M.A. Secondary Education, concentration in Alternative Education, December 1999
 San Francisco State University, San Francisco, California

B.A. History and Psychology Majors, English and Math Minors, July 1997
 Stanford University, Stanford, California

PART-TIME EMPLOYMENT AND INTERESTS

Web page developer and computer programmer, Bay Electronics, 1996-present
Piano and bass teacher, private instruction, San Francisco Bay Area, 1995-present
Acoustical and electric bass performer and manager of Bay Jazz
Piano; composing music; playing baseball and working at youth camps

References available at Teacher Career Center, Any City, State 12345 (101) 555-0008

VISUAL FEATURES

Word processing or desktop publishing allows you to design a format that fits your needs and to select layout features to enhance your message. Variable sizes of print can make your résumé interesting and reader friendly as well as allow you to emphasize section headings, important assignments, or specific preparations. Scalable fonts available with personal computers make it possible to design an eye-catching résumé that subtly draws the reader's attention to the points you wish to highlight.

Don't get carried away with variety for variety's sake. Efficient communication depends on the twin goals of clarity and legibility. Unusual fonts such as "olde Englishe" or script or shadowed letters can be distracting, and even irritating. Keep your choices few, simple, and meaningful.

Hints:

- Nothing should be larger than your name.

- Section headings should be of uniform size.

- Annotations can appear less formidable and take up less of your valuable space if they use a slightly smaller font.

- Overuse of large print wastes space and time, because it slows the reader's eye, and may look like an attempt to stretch limited information.

ACCENTS AND EMPHASIS

Computer technology has made it very easy to add designs, figures, clip art, or drawings to a résumé. A note of caution regarding graphic enhancement is in order, however. Intricate patterns, cute figures, or large, bold designs appear gimmicky and draw attention away from the message of the résumé. In addition, if the potential employer's scanning technology does not readily accept graphics, the appearance and readability of your résumé is in jeopardy.

Design your résumé to direct the reader's attention to your strong points. Choose features that intensify the visual impact and improve the communication ability of your résumé. Simple techniques can achieve attractive and professional results. For example, a small bullet (•) or dash (-) can draw attention to a special item or unify similar entries:

- Elected student body president

- Nominated for Teacher of the Year

- Selected Rhodes Scholar regional finalist

Section headings can be accented with **bold** print or CAPITAL LETTERS, making the divisions of your résumé more prominent. *Italic print* can be used for emphasis, or simply for variety. Overuse of any of these accent techniques will diminish their effect.

WHITE SPACE

A judicious use of white space creates a layout that is both attractive and easy to read. White space makes your résumé far more inviting than a cramped, dense block of text bristling with dates and locations. Ample margins, extra spaces between sections, indentation, and the use of columns can all contribute to an airy and accessible effect.

7

THE
FINAL
PRODUCT

As you approach the final stages of résumé preparation, you must become not only a writer but an editor. If you were writing for publication, you would have the luxury of working with an editor who could read your work with a clear and objective eye. The editor would catch inaccuracies and inconsistencies. Problems arising from ambiguities, extraneous language, and faulty organization would be spotted and resolved.

These editorial functions must be performed before your résumé is ready for production. If you are persuasive enough, you might talk someone else into editing your résumé for you. With or without assistance, you have ultimate responsibility for the final product. No one is in a better position to make editorial decisions about the relevance of each entry, the importance of individual word selection, and the effect created by the arrangement of the material.

Perhaps the most difficult aspect of editing your own material is deciding what to cut out. Everything you have put into your draft is there because it seems relevant. As a beginning teacher or a veteran with years of experience, you have to challenge the significance of each item, to question whether its contribution justifies the space it requires. Sometimes you can compromise; sometimes you simply have to be ruthless in your actions.

PROOFREADING

After you have drafted, revised, and edited your résumé, there is one more step before you are ready to produce the genuine article. That important step is proofreading. Never neglect or underestimate the importance of proofreading

One simple mistake can be disastrous. Take the time to check each word for spelling and each entry for accuracy, grammar, and punctuation. Make full use of a computer's spell-checker if you can, but don't rely on it completely. It won't recognize a misplaced or misused word if it is spelled correctly.

You have the ultimate responsibility for the document, but you probably will not be the best proofreader. After you have written, rewritten, chopped, added, cut and pasted, thrown it away and started over, you will very likely see what you expect to see. Get help from friends, colleagues, roommates, instructors—anyone who is willing and reasonably knowledgeable—even Uncle Jack. Make any necessary changes or corrections, then move into the production stage.

PRODUCTION

The availability of campus computer systems and of personal computers has made dramatic changes in the way most résumés are produced. Tailoring a résumé to meet the requirements of a specific job, rearranging categories to highlight particularly appropriate skills or experiences, or simply updating and changing an address is quickly and easily accomplished

Print Quality. Any printer can give you a draft version so you can begin to see how your résumé will look. For the final version, only a clear, sharp image is acceptable. A good printer can give you a finished copy that is ready to represent you as a professional. If you have access to a letter-quality printer, you can produce copies as you need them. If your printer cannot provide the quality you desire, or if you do not have access to a printer, commercial printing businesses can process your résumé from your diskette.

Special Note: Professional papers are not handwritten. You may have the most sophisticated handwriting, you may print beautifully, or you may even be a master of calligraphy, but your résumé is not the place to demonstrate these abilities. It is also unprofessional and unadvisable to make handwritten corrections, additions, or updates to a conventionally produced résumé.

MULTIPLE PAGES

If your résumé consists of more than one page, each page after the first should be numbered. Your name should appear on every page. Do not fasten the pages together with staples or clips and never print on both sides of the page.

Presentations on 11 × 17-inch paper, folded in half to create a brochure effect, are difficult to scan or to copy. Because they require a minimum of two full pages of text, they are unsuitable for nearly all beginning teachers, who may attempt to fill a brochure with large fonts, extra spacing, or extraneous descriptions. Even for experienced professionals, the brochure offers no clear advantage.

PAPER SELECTION

The paper you select for your résumé contributes to your professional image. It does not have to be the most expensive stock available, but it should be at least 20-pound bond. Standard size for a professional resume is 8½ × 11 inches. Larger or smaller paper is usually more of a nuisance than an asset; it doesn't stack or file properly, and it cannot be copied as readily.

The exact weight or texture of the paper you select is a matter of personal taste, but anything truly unusual should be avoided. Similarly, the use of colored stock is a legitimate option. Soft tints in neutral colors are acceptable and can be attractive. Bright colors will, indeed, attract attention, but perhaps not the kind of attention you want to receive. Plain white paper is always a viable option for creating a crisp, professional image.

Using the same paper for your correspondence with employers is a good idea. Matching envelopes are a nice added touch, though the envelope is often discarded immediately upon opening.

THE FINAL REVIEW

Never submit a résumé that does not represent your best interests. Any of the following flaws could be fatal to your chances:

- Lack of focus or direction
- Long, rambling sentences
- Use of personal pronoun
- Dense blocks of narrative
- Poor print quality (light, faded)
- Inconsistent format

Anything less than perfection will detract from your overall impression. Evidence of carelessness in producing or handling the document—any smudge, stain, dog-eared corner, or unnecessary crease or fold—is grounds for immediate rejection.

A good-looking résumé will get you noticed; you get only one chance to make a good impression.

ELECTRONIC AND MULTIMEDIA RESUMES

The electronic age adds new dimensions to a job search, introducing new technology, new terminology, new acronyms, and untold jargon:

- WWW, BBSs, URL, TIFF

- Nodes, net, links, bits, and bytes

- GIF, HTML, ASCII, and http

These are common terms to many people, new-age gibberish to some.

Without a doubt, electronic résumés are playing a growing and increasingly important role in the marketplace. Cyberspace is no longer science fiction and today's educators have new opportunities and new avenues to conduct a job search.

Whether you submit your résumé on paper or through an electronic medium, employers need basic information about your educational background and experiences. The content—though not necessarily the appearance—of your paper résumé can translate directly into an electronic version. You can create a résumé with any standard word processing application or a specialized software package that leads you through a step-by-step process of constructing a résumé.

Submitting your résumé to an employer using electronic mail (E-mail) typically requires that you first save your document as "text only" in an ASCII file. ASCII is the acronym for American Standard Code of Information Interchange, a format that recognizes only text. Formatting codes, graphics, some punctuation marks, special fonts, and highlighting features, for example, boldface, italics, underlining, are not compatible with current ASCII features. For this reason, you will need to start your category headings at the left margin. It is possible to indent or to separate category headings from the descriptive information by adding spaces. ASCII will not recognize a centered format.

SCREEN IMAGE

When your résumé appears on a computer screen, you do not have the same opportunity to control the overall appearance as you do with a conventional paper résumé. Keep in mind that with standard E-mail transmission, the first four or five lines of the screen consist of header information: date and time, your name and E-mail address, the recipient's E-mail address, and a subject line.

The subject line is important. Use it to state the purpose of the message quickly and clearly. Be sure to follow any specific instructions provided by the employer in a job advertisement or an employment application. If no instructions have been provided, be direct and professional, for example, English Résumé, Résumé of Bilingual Kindergarten Teacher, Employment Résumé—Elementary Principal.

Only a limited portion of your résumé will appear on the screen, so it is imperative that the first or initial screen tell the reader about your employment interests. If your standard paper résumé does not lead off with this information, you will need to rearrange or perhaps create a category to communicate clearly your skills and competencies. Another change you will need to make on your electronic résumé concerns the placement of your address and other contact information. In order to have your name and your job objective or teaching interests appear on the first screen, you can move your contact information to the bottom of your page.

```
Date: Tue,22May1999 22:27:39-0500(CDT)
From: Ima Sample <imasample@blue.weeg.anyuniv.edu>
To: hiring-official@anyschool.edu
Subject: Alternative high school candidate


IMA SAMPLE
Alternative High School Instructor
    -Academic strengths in English, History, Math,
     Psychology
    -Student-Centered Approach with Emphasis on Goal
     Setting
    -Strong Collaborative Skills
```

The length of your résumé is perhaps even more important when the reader is required to scroll or page down in order to view the complete document. A traditional one-page paper résumé may fill three screens; after three or four screens, the reader's interest and patience begin to diminish. If your electronic version necessitates viewing many screens, you need to cut it.

Length is not the only issue. A dense block of text looks cramped and formidable. As you edit your résumé, don't sacrifice an open, inviting format by crowding each screen.

Avoid attention-getting gimmicks such as "smileys" :) or other graphic representations constructed from standard keystrokes. These devices are inappropriate—regardless of the medium—for what remains a standard business communication between professionals.

ELECTRONIC HEADINGS

Because you are unable to highlight your résumé with italics, bold accents, or different fonts, capital letters are the only device you can employ to give emphasis to your text. The best use of capitals is for category headings. In E-mail conventions, capital letters within the text are considered rude, the typographic equivalent of shouting in the middle of a conversation.

Date: Tue,22May1999 22:27:39-0500(CDT)
From: Ima Sample <imasample@blue.weeg.anyuniv.edu>
To: hiring-official@anyschool.edu
Subject: Resume of Elementary Art Teacher

IMA SAMPLE

TEACHING SKILLS	Art teacher - elementary grades, K-6 -Special expertise in painting, sculpture, and multimedia -Experience with integrated lessons in collaborative settings -Extensive technology skills and 3-D graphic design
EDUCATION	B.F.A. Seattle University, May 1999 International Study in Milan and Florence, Italy, 1998 The Kansas City Art Institute, 1995-1997
STUDENT INTERNSHIP	Elementary Art, Pacific Coast Elementary, Seattle, Spring 1999 K-6 diverse classrooms with inclusion philosophy. Lessons include bookmaking, puppetmaking, printmaking, weaving, metalsmithing, and multimedia. Integrated lessons to reflect everyday activities for all learners in collaborative setting.
ART FIELD EXPERIENCES	Middle School & K-3 Art, Seattle Public Schools, Spring 1998 Prepared lessons in ceramics, drawing, painting, calligraphy, mixed-media, and special research projects. Guided an outdoor education art workshop for a team retreat. Joined in child study teams. Organized several art shows and contests.

RECOGNITION	Academic:
	    Scholastic Art Award, Gold Key and Blue Ribbon
	    Frank Jesper Scholarship to Kansas City Art Institute
	
	Art:
	Group Show: Missouri Arts Show, Kansas City Art Center, 1999
	Juried Show: 40th Annual Seattle Artist's Show, Seattle, 1998
	Invitational Exhibition: Pacific Coast Invitational, 1997

CONTACT	Ima Sample, 221 College Street, Any City, State 12345 (101)555-0009(home) (101)522-0099(campus)
PORTFOLIO REFERENCES	Complete teaching portfolio available for review. Education Placement Office, Any City, State 12345 (101)555-0008

YOUR RESUME AND THE WORLD WIDE WEB

The Internet and the World Wide Web present yet another marketing opportunity for educators seeking new positions. Designing a résumé for the World Wide Web demands the same careful attention to relevance and professionalism as a conventional résumé.

Résumés created in Hypertext Markup Language (HTML) offer opportunities to incorporate features not available in any other format. Images, sounds, video, and links to other Web sites can all be built into a multimedia résumé. The potential for creativity offered by this medium is practically unlimited. You can use this technology to build an electronic portfolio and a personal home page dealing with a variety of your interests. This is the place to demonstrate your technology skills by incorporating color, action, sound, and graphic design features.

The most effective Web résumé presents your skills, abilities, and training unencumbered by extraneous material.

- Job seekers should never provide personal data or photographs to potential employers.

- Avoid informal chat or lingo.

- Resist dark or heavily patterned backgrounds.

- Using clip art is unoriginal and unnecessary. "Borrowing" cartoons or other copyrighted material is unprofessional and illegal.

- Provide links only to your E-mail address and to sites containing material you have created (lesson plans, philosophy statement).

Consider your Web résumé a supplement to the résumé you have already created for paper or E-mail submission. It need not be a replica of your initial résumé. You can expand on some categories and minimize others and you can provide a link to your own electronic portfolio.

Put your address of your Web site or URL (Uniform Resource Locator) on the résumé you use to introduce yourself to potential employers. Your URL can appear with your address at the top of the paper résumé or at the bottom of your E-mail version.

SURVIVING THE SCANNER

Scanning technology used for recruitment and screening purposes, however, sophisticated, has two simple purposes: to enter your résumé into a database and to sort for keywords significant to the employer. School districts may have any number of terms entered into their database, and the keywords they use are determined by their needs, their philosophies, their educational goals, and the demographics of the community.

Provide clear and specific information about your skills and experiences. For example, if you describe yourself as bilingual, you may increase your chances of being selected by the scanner if you add qualifiers such as "bilingual—Spanish/English" or "bilingual—Hmong and English."

Scanning software does not read graphics, including diamonds, bullets, check marks, horizontal or vertical lines, or text boxes. Scanners read standard fonts such as Courier or Helvetica without difficulty, but may not recognize other font styles.

Textured or colored paper stock is also problematic. To be on the safe side, use ordinary white paper, a standard font, black print, and no graphics. This plain, ungarnished document may not have the visual interest of your paper résumé, but it will survive the scanner and allow you to be considered for available positions.

EMPLOYER EXPECTATIONS ABOUT RESUMES

Whether they are holding your résumé in their hand or reading it on a computer screen, hiring officials have a limited amount of time to make preliminary or first-round selections. Screening can be based solely on a quick glance at your résumé and cover letter. It doesn't take long to make decisions—maybe thirty seconds, maybe even less. Surprising as it may seem, your résumé and your future can be related to a stack labeled *Yes, No,* or *Maybe* on the basis of a rapidly formed opinion.

Very few principals or superintendents would consider themselves experts in the art of constructing a résumé. In the limited amount of time they can devote to the screening process, they make quick, hard decisions based on the following simple criteria:

- Neat, fresh, legible, and error-free résumé
- Clearly identified teaching field, skills, strengths
- Effective language and correct grammar
- Positive and promising professional image

Surviving this initial screening is critical but it is not particularly difficult. Avoiding the *No* bin, the wastebasket, or the Delete key demands that your paper or electronic image be convincing, relevant, and positive.

TAILORING YOUR RESUME

A résumé should be designed to accomplish a specific purpose; in other words, your résumé must fit the job. Tailoring a résumé for specific jobs can be easily accomplished. By rearranging categories, highlighting the most relevant experiences or qualifications, adding or deleting details, you can target a specific job. Personal computers make this a simple task.

For example, if you are certified to teach social studies, you will probably start with a résumé that presents your qualifications as a generalist. As opportunities arise, modifications can be made to reflect your preparation in such specific areas as American history, government, world history, or international affairs.

A music teacher, for example, may be licensed to work with students from kindergarten through twelfth grade in general and vocal music. One résumé could emphasize preparation and experience for working with high school choral groups; another version could concentrate on a general music program for elementary students.

A RESUME IS NOT AN ALL-PURPOSE DOCUMENT

Your employment résumé addresses skills, strengths, competencies, extracurricular interests, and educational background. If you are seeking two distinctly different kinds of positions, such as classroom teacher and school principal, you need to prepare more than one résumé. Obviously, these positions have different responsibilities; they require different preparations and different skills. A teaching résumé, however well prepared, will send the wrong message in an administrative search: It could imply that you are insufficiently aware of the differences between teaching and administration, that you have not given enough thought to changing jobs, or that you are simply a poor communicator.

RESUMES FOR OTHER PURPOSES

Perhaps the most widely recognized use of a résumé is in the employment process, but educators will find many other situations in which a résumé can be a useful tool:

• Evaluations/performance reviews

- Grant proposals

- Applications for special honors, awards

- Conference presentations

- Candidacy for election to office in a professional association

- Background material for the person who introduces you as a speaker or panel member

A résumé used for general introductions presents experiences, leadership roles, recognitions, and other accomplishments selected and arranged for their relevance. For example, if you are to present a paper or a talk at a professional conference, you might be asked to provide background information to the person who will introduce you. You would prepare a different résumé for the person who will introduce your address to a local service club. See examples on pages 115 and 156.

Similarly, you might find it necessary to prepare a résumé for a performance review or evaluation, to accompany a grant application, or to provide information when you are a candidate for office in a professional association. A résumé can also be helpful in support of your nomination or application for an award. Each of these occasions requires a customized résumé that could be quite different from the résumé sent to a potential employer. The content, the arrangement, and the emphasis must be directed toward the proper goal.

Note: Shortcuts won't work. Take time to prepare different versions. Your résumé must be appropriate for the purpose.

10
RESUMES FOR ADMINISTRATORS

Candidates for an administrative position at the building or central office level need to craft a résumé specifically targeted for the available position, carefully outlining educational training, specific skills, and accumulated experiences. The most effective résumés for educators in administrative or supervisory roles focus on competencies and experiences directly related to immediate objectives.

In current practice, an administrator's résumé will be carefully reviewed by many different people involved in the selection process, from school board officials to community representatives. Acronyms, abbreviations, technical terminology, and currently fashionable catchwords should be avoided or used very sparingly. The content of your résumé must be comprehensible to people who are not trained educators, yet sufficiently detailed to be meaningful to practicing professionals.

NEW ADMINISTRATORS

A teacher seeking an entry-level administrative position must demonstrate successful teaching experiences as well as leadership capabilities and responsibilities assumed in school or community projects. Service or leadership at the department, building, or district level illustrates interest, commitment, and involvement.

Key items for a new administrator's résumé:

- Evidence of academic training in educational administration
- Identified professional strengths and abilities
- Documented experience as a successful teacher
- Manifest commitment to students, colleagues, and the learning community

EXPERIENCED ADMINISTRATORS

If you are a veteran administrator, a complete list of your activities and responsibilities over the years could produce a document running to several single-spaced pages. For maximum impact, priorities must be assigned in order to trim your résumé to a manageable size. Editing—selecting, summarizing, and condensing your career experiences and achievements into an effective promotional package—could be your most difficult task.

In addition to an employment history, experienced administrators should provide evidence of current and continuing development. Membership in professional associations is expected; presentations, recognitions, or positions of responsibility at the local, regional, or national level should be highlighted.

Key items for experienced administrators are:

- Evidence of building staff and community consensus in support of district goals

- Management skills in finance, enrollment, and diversity issues

- Proficiency in administrative and instructional technology

- Exemplary leadership in curriculum, and commitment to academic success for all students

An effective way to demonstrate your past achievements is to design a résumé section or even a special page entitled Professional Activities and Accomplishments. Topics to consider including are:

- Curriculum Development

- Committee Leadership

- Strategic Planning

- Staff Development and In-service

- Financial Management

- Policy Development

- District Initiatives

- Grant Writing

- Building Referendums

- Selected Presentations

- Professional Service

PROFESSIONAL ACTIVITIES AND ACCOMPLISHMENTS

COMMITTEE LEADERSHIP
Management Technology Committee-Chair 1999-present
Community/School Partnerships-Co-Chair 1999-present
Technology Committee-District Facilitator...1998-present
Curriculum for 2000 Committee-Facilitator..1998-present
Professional Growth Committee-Chair 1997-present
Salary Negotiations Committee-Co-Chair..1995-present

POLICY DEVELOPMENT
Developed policies, procedures, and regulations required for implementation for the following:

Civil Rights	Affirmative Action	Drug-Free Workplace	Family and Medical Leave
Continuing Contract	Professional Growth	Budget Development	New Facilities Construction

GRANT WRITING
Initiated and secured state and federal monies through three grant proposals to begin programs in technology training for professionals and classroom teaching, career education/school-to-work initiatives, and in gifted education, 1996-1999.

Grant proposal in process entitled "School-to Work Technology Training for Urban Alternative Centers." Submitted to Department of Education, Washington D.C., Fall 1999.

DISTRICT INITIATIVES
Designed, coordinated, and supervised a lifelong learning program that maximizes the effectiveness of people, programs, and facilities for the benefit of all citizens in the school district. Planned a Continuing Adult Education Program and evaluated all phases of the program for reports to the State Department, local advisory council, and school board officials.

Planned and implemented a three-year professional staff induction and orientation program currently used throughout the district and as a Department of Education model for districts within the state.

Developed the philosophical and conceptual framework and directed the process for establishing a technology plan for managerial personnel in district of over 14,000 students.

SELECTED PRESENTATIONS
"School-to-Work Initiatives: Developing Programs That Work," National Association for Alternative Schools Conference, Chicago, Illinois, May 1999.

"Parent and Guardian Partnerships in Career Development," Northeast Association of School Boards National Roundtable, Brattleboro, Vermont, April 1998.

"Managing Data Using Federal Guidelines," American Association for School Personnel Administrators National Conference, Portland, Oregon, October 1997.

Complete list of presentations, committee responsibilities, and
community and professional service available upon request.

An overview of professional experience at the beginning of the résumé can be particularly helpful to the reader. It provides a quick summary of your career progression and establishes a framework for the entire presentation.

- Assistant Superintendent   3 years
- High School Principal   6 years
- Assistant Principal   2 years
- Classroom Teacher   5 years

For administrators at any level, accuracy is paramount; any error, inconsistency, or misrepresentation will prove damaging if not fatal. An attractive, purposeful résumé will enhance your image as a dynamic, knowledgeable leader.

11

RESUMES FOR INTERNATIONAL TEACHING

A specialized résumé will be essential if you are seeking a teaching position in another country. International schools are looking for people who are flexible, adaptable, and independent. A résumé that reflects these essential qualities, and portrays you as a versatile educator who can contribute to several different areas of school life will immediately catch the international employer's attention.

Tailor your international résumé carefully, and consider it a single-purpose document. There are a few adjustments you will need to make on a résumé that is designed solely for international opportunities. In addition to presenting your credentials, focus on skills and attributes that have special significance for international hiring officials.

GENUINE RESUME ASSETS

Foreign Language Ability
In American-sponsored international schools, the language of instruction will be English. You need not be fluent in the language of the host country to be considered for employment. However, knowledge of any foreign language will contribute to your ability to learn the language of your new community and will make for an easier transition.

International Experience
Previous experience of living and/or studying in another country will be viewed positively by prospective employers. If you spent a summer, a semester, or an academic year abroad, be sure to include all relevant information. Exchange students who have the advantage of living with a host family may have an easier adjustment to living in a new setting.

Travel
Experienced travelers are more likely to adjust quickly to a new setting. Even a limited exposure to different cultures, new surroundings, and unfamiliar customs will usually lessen the severity and shorten the duration of the inevitable culture shock.

Related Interests

A demonstrated commitment to learning about other cultures and a concern for international affairs can be displayed on your résumé by stating membership in various kinds of international clubs or associations, volunteer service as a guide, language partner, or "friend" to foreign students, or even by elective courses in relevant ethnic, cultural, or area studies.

Other Interests

Leisure time can pose problems for people who depend on activities or resources not universally available. Avocations (photography, philately, sketching, reading, needlework, writing, hiking, and sightseeing) that can be pursued independently and without group or family support provide yet another indication of probable success in adjusting to a strange environment.

CITIZENSHIP AND OTHER DATA

A special section of your résumé should be devoted to personal information including citizenship, marital status, and number of dependents who would accompany you. It is not necessary to include vital statistics (age, height, weight, religion, or ethnic identity). (See résumés in the International Settings section, beginning on page 168.) Unlike stateside hiring officials, directors of international schools may have a genuine need to be aware of your marital status and number of dependents. In some locations, housing suitable for families is simply not available. Only single teachers or a teaching couple with no dependent children can be considered for employment. The extreme difficulty or sheer impossibility of obtaining a work permit for a nonteaching spouse can also make it necessary for employers to hire only teaching couples or single teachers.

12

RESUMES FOR NONCERTIFIED TEACHERS

The traditional route to a career in education is through a teacher preparation program leading to licensure or certification. Even without a teaching license, it is possible to explore employment opportunities in schools and other settings.

Independent Schools

Some states do not require state certification for teachers in nonpublic or independent schools, a classification that can include preparatory schools, boarding schools, and parochial schools. Independent schools may offer internship or teaching fellowship opportunities for first-year teachers. Typically, a fellowship provides a stipend rather than a full salary.

English Language Instruction

Language centers around the world employ native speakers as instructors of conversational English. Major corporations and educational institutions in South America, Africa, Asia, and Eastern Europe hire college graduates interested in living and teaching in a different environment and culture. Teaching experience and certification are not required. Although advertisements frequently refer to ESL, TOEFL, or TESOL, teaching positions may not require specific training in English or linguistics.

Preschools

Preschool and day care centers afford opportunities for college students and for college graduates who are interested in working with young children. Teaching certificates are not typically required, although some states license head teachers or directors of day care centers.

Learning Centers and Agencies

Private agencies provide tutoring and special assistance to students at various levels, from young children to adult learners. Depending on the center's philosophy or mission, the instruction may be geared toward developmental or accelerated learning. These agencies hire both certified teachers and noncertified teachers with a strong academic background in the tutorial area.

Health Care Facilities

Educational departments or divisions for pediatric patients exist in nearly all major hospitals. Individuals work with long-term patients or homebound students in virtually all subject areas. Some opportunities exist for instructors or tutors who are not licensed teachers.

Alternative Routes to Certification

A number of states have implemented alternative routes to certification. Provisional or substandard certificates can be issued for college graduates who lack required course work and practicum experience. Some states issue provisional certificates only in areas where there is a severe shortage of licensed teachers. In other states, alternative routes to certification may be possible in any teaching field.

RELEVANT HIGHLIGHTS

Information about preprofessional activities, such as student teaching or practicum experiences, is an important resume section for licensed teachers. Noncertified teachers must concentrate on other experiences that highlight related background, appropriate skills, and demonstrated abilities.

Special attention must be given to selecting, assigning priorities, and arranging résumé items. The same person could conceivably prepare a résumé for teaching either in a preschool or a college preparatory school. Much of the information would be the same; however, sections of the résumé could be modified to emphasize different skills and experiences.

- Experience with appropriate age groups

- Volunteer activities

- Personal attributes

- Relevant course work

- Special skills

- Cultural awareness

- Travel

- Language skills

- Involvement/Activism

- Leadership

13
EFFECTIVE COVER LETTERS

Even the greatest soloist usually require an accompanist. Your best résumé, too, will need a companion piece—usually called a cover letter.

Writing a good basic cover letter is much easier than preparing a résumé. You have fewer choices to worry about; there are simple conventions for standard business letters, and you should follow them.

For cover letters submitted by conventional means (on paper and delivered by mail):

- Use standard 8½ × 11-inch stationery, preferably the same paper stock you have chosen for your résumé.

- Use only one side of the page.

- The return address and the date should appear at the top of the page.

- The inside address (name and title of the individual, name and address of the institution) should appear at least three spaces before the date and flush with the left margin.

- The body of the letter should be single-spaced, with double spacing between paragraphs.

- Paragraphs may begin at the left margin or five spaces to the right.

- The complimentary close should appear two spaces below the last line of the letter.

- Leave four spaces between the complimentary close and your name to allow for your signature.

- The word "enclosure" appears two or more spaces below your name when you include additional items, for example, résumé, transcripts, application form.

BEYOND THE MECHANICS—OR, WHAT DO I WRITE?

Start at the beginning. You cannot go wrong by clearly stating the purpose of your letter in your opening sentence—or at least early in the first paragraph. Because many school districts have a number of positions available, a clear statement of why you are writing will allow the employer to process your application efficiently.

Once the opening lines are out of the way, go on to the main idea. In a letter of application for employment, this means pointing out specific qualifications and experiences directly related to the available position. Highlight relevant experiences, emphasize appropriate training, and sell yourself as a competent and committed professional. This middle section or the concluding paragraph of your letter can provide information about supporting documents such as references or transcripts.

A letter of application should always include some reference to the next step in the process—the interview. You may request an appointment directly or use a slightly more subtle phrase such as, "I am very interested in this position and look forward to discussing it with you," but let the reader know that you want to arrange an interview.

Outside of education, job seekers are encouraged to be direct and assertive about the next step. Frequently, a letter concludes with a statement such as, "I will call you next Thursday to arrange an interview." This approach may work in some business fields, but it is not appropriate for educators. Because selection processes in education involve extensive paper screening, employers will initiate the arrangements for interviews.

COMMUNICATION IS THE GOAL

The ability to write clear, elegant prose is certainly an asset, but you don't have to be a great writer to produce a good letter. And you don't have to get writer's block when you sit down to compose a cover letter.

Complete sentences grouped in cohesive paragraphs are all that is required. Pay careful attention to spelling, grammar, and punctuation. Keep your language professional; resist any temptation to inflate your vocabulary in order to sound more intellectual or knowledgeable. No literary prizes are at stake; all you need to do is convey your message clearly and correctly.

SAMPLE COVER LETTER

221 College Street
Any City, State 12345
March 28, 1999

Lee Smith, Ph.D.
Superintendent
Anyplace School District
City, State 12347

Dear Dr. Smith:

Please consider me as an applicant for the high school language arts opening currently being advertised by Anyplace School District. I recently learned of your teaching opening from the Educational Placement Office at Central State University where I will earn my bachelor's degree in May of this year with a major in English and a minor in journalism and mass communication.

As the enclosed résumé indicates, I am completing a full semester internship at City High School working with a diverse student population in grades nine through twelve. In addition to my classroom experiences teaching British Literature, Twentieth Century American Authors, and ninth grade Basic English, I volunteer to work individually and in small groups with the school's newspaper staff. I am particularly interested in your advertised opening because of the specific teaching responsibilities and the opportunity to advise the student magazine and work with other student publications.

As your advertisement instructs, I have completed the school district's application on the World Wide Web and am currently arranging for Central University's Registrar's Office to submit my transcripts to you. My letters of recommendation are being sent from the Educational Placement Office. I would welcome the opportunity to interview with your selection team and I look forward to hearing from you in the near future.

Sincerely,

Ima Sample

Enclosure

PART TWO

SAMPLE
RESUMES

14
MAKING THE
BEST USE OF
THESE SAMPLES

If you do nothing more than page through the following samples, find the one that most closely matches your teaching area, and plug in your own information, you'll have an acceptable résumé. It might even look as good as most of the others in the stack on the employer's desk.

But it won't be the best résumé you could create. You don't have to settle for just a satisfactory appearance. Your résumé can do more than merely convey information to someone else; it can help you identify and concentrate on your particular strengths and interests, and organize your thoughts in preparation for interviews.

Take the time to read Part I of this book so you will understand how to capitalize on your strengths and abilities and how to convey these strengths and abilities to potential employers. Once you have read the introductory material, you will see how the samples work. You will understand how to highlight a special skill, how to emphasize a particular experience, and how to minimize events or circumstances that could be perceived as liabilities.

The sample résumés represent a wide variety of teaching interests, fields, specializations, and experiences. It would be natural to start with the one that seems to be the closest match. Before you adopt this résumé as your model, however, look at several others. You may find one in a different teaching field that is better suited to your particular situation.

Don't hesitate to combine elements of different samples. You might choose the layout from one, the category headings from another (with your own modifications), the font or typeface from a third, a graphic from yet another. You can borrow, incorporate, or adapt from any number of samples to create your personal résumé.

Add your own touches as well. The final product will represent you as a distinctive individual:

- an educator with an awareness of teaching capabilities and special strengths;

- an educator with recognized talents and accomplishments; and

- an educator who demonstrates personal commitment and professional purpose.

15

BEGINNING TEACHERS

WILL B. GOODE

221 College Street, Any City, State 12345 (101) 555-0009
will-goode@seatuniv.edu

TEACHING SKILLS
Art teacher - elementary grades, K-6
Special expertise in painting, sculpture, and multimedia
Experience in designing integrated lessons in collaborative settings
Technology skills in graphic design and various software applications

EDUCATION
B.F.A. Seattle University, May 1999
International Study in Milan and Florence, Italy, 1998
The Kansas City Art Institute, 1995-1997

STUDENT INTERNSHIP
Elementary Art, Pacific Coast Elementary, Seattle, Spring 1999
Teaching responsibilities include working with students in all K-6 classrooms. Lessons include bookmaking, painting, drawing, puppetmaking, printmaking, weaving, metalsmithing, and multimedia. Integrated lessons to reflect everyday activities and to include topics in science and social studies. Created projects for all learners from inclusion students to non-English speakers. Helped students display artwork in storefronts, local office buildings, and Seattle Children's Museum.

ART FIELD EXPERIENCES
Middle School and K-3 Art, Seattle Public Schools, Fall 1998
Prepared lessons in ceramics, drawing, painting, calligraphy, mixed-media, and special research projects. Guided an outdoor education art workshop for a team retreat. Joined in child study teams and was available for after-school help on a daily basis. Organized several art shows and contests.

RECOGNITION
Academic:
Scholastic Art Award, Gold Key, and Blue Ribbon
Frank Jesper Scholarship to Kansas City Art Institute

Art:
Group Show: Missouri Arts Show, Kansas City Art Center, 1999
Juried Show: 40th Annual Seattle Artist's Show, Seattle, 1998
Invitational Exhibition: Pacific Coast Invitational, Vancouver, 1997

PORTFOLIO AND REFERENCES
Complete portfolio available for review.
Education Placement Office, Any City, State 12345 (101) 555-0008

ROSE LARA

221 College Street
Any City, State 12345
(101) 555-0009

TEACHING OBJECTIVE
Bilingual Kindergarten Teacher

STRENGTHS
Multicultural teaching experience
Fluent in Spanish
Trained in early childhood developmental philosophy
Understand the educational needs of at-risk students

TEACHING EXPERIENCE
Natchitoches Preschool Center, Natchitoches, Louisiana, Spring 1999
Kindergarten & Prekindergarten Intern

Responsibilities in the five-month internship include:
- Develop and conduct classroom lessons in both Spanish and English
- Reinforce material by involving non-English speaking parents in the classroom and school activities
- Write and implement IEP's for each student and review with parents in school or home-based conferences
- Work extensively with individual students in beginning reading program
- Use cultural activities, songs, and materials to enhance learning and self-esteem

CLASSROOM EXPERIENCES
Cloutierville Elementary School, Cloutierville, Louisiana, Fall 1998
Transitional First Grade Practicum

Goldonna Elementary School, Goldonna, Louisiana, Summer 1997
First Grade Reading Recovery Program Observation

North Natchitoches Elementary School, Natchitoches, Louisiana, Spring 1996
Bilingual Kindergarten Practicum

COLLEGE ACTIVITIES
Member, Gamma Phi Beta Sorority - Newsletter Editor, Pledge Director, Treasurer
Player/coach, Intramural Basketball; volunteer referee and timekeeper
Board Member, Student Activities Council
Co-chair, Dragon Boat Festival

COMMUNITY SERVICE
Habitat for Humanity Volunteer, St. Tammany and Lafourche Parishes, Louisiana
Spring breaks and summers, present. Work with student and adult volunteers from
various parts of the country to rebuild homes for families in need.

EDUCATIONAL BACKGROUND
Northwestern State University, Natchitoches, Louisiana
Bachelor of Arts Degree, May 1998 Major: Early Childhood; Minor: ESL

CREDENTIALS
Education Placement Office, Any City, State 12345
Telephone: (101) 555-0008   FAX: (101) 555-0089

ANNA HANSEN

221 College Street
Any City, State 12345
(101) 555-0009

OBJECTIVE

Teacher: Early Childhood Education
Preschool Education

EDUCATION

University of Utah, Salt Lake City, Utah
B.A. Degree - May, 1999
Major: Early Childhood Education
Area of Specialization: Psychology

COURSE HIGHLIGHTS

Educational Psychology   Early Childhood Teaching
Language and Society   Multicultural-Bilingual Education
Child Development   Spanish I-IV

STUDENT TEACHING

Early Childhood Center, Head Start Center, Pioneer, Utah, 9/98-12/98

Responsibilities:
• Instructed a diverse student population including ESL students
• Taught individualized math using manipulatives
• Organized and created learning centers and bulletin boards
• Used cooperative learning strategies
• Introduced computer use in learning centers
• Provided students with individualized attention
• Created flannel board stories to enhance learning
• Kept concise records of students' progress
• Worked productively with staff, students, and parents

Pre-Kindergarten, Jensen Elementary, Salt Lake City, Utah, 1/99-4/99

Responsibilities:
• Developed learning stations in reading and science
• Taught reading to a small group of beginning readers
• Designed and maintained progress charts
• Worked closely with three disabled children
• Communicated with parents on a regular basis
• Attended child study team meetings and staffing for
  learning disabled

RELATED ACTIVITIES

Hospital tutor, University of Utah Medical Center, summer, 1995-1997
HACAP volunteer, Hooper Community Center, Hooper, Utah, 1993-1995
Swim instructor, Civic Center, Grantsville, Utah, 1993-1995
Member, National Association for Young Children

CREDENTIALS

Career Planning & Placement
Any City, State 12345 Telephone: (101) 555-0008

DEVIN ANDREWS

Present Address:
221 College Street
Any City, State 12345
(101) 555-0009

Permanent Address:
30 Royal Avenue
Mytown, State 23456
(909) 333-0003

TEACHING INTERESTS
- Primary Grades (K-3) - Reading Recovery Experience - At-Risk Training

COACHING INTERESTS
- Soccer - all levels - Assist in basketball, track - Coaching authorization - State of Idaho

ACADEMIC BACKGROUND
Idaho State University, Pocatello, Idaho B.A. Degree, 7/99 Major: Elementary Education
Dean's List, Idaho State University *Tuition Scholarship* *Jacob's Senior Award*

STUDENT TEACHING EXPERIENCE
First Grade-Reading Recovery Program, Towers Elementary, Boise, Idaho Public Schools, 3/99 to 5/99
Kindergarten and Transitional First Grade, Briggs Elementary, Boise, Idaho Public Schools, 1/99 to 3/99
Early Childhood and Preschool Training Program, Department of Defense, Munich, Germany, Summer '99
Responsibilities during the above teaching positions included:
- Planning developmentally appropriate activites following weekly themes and organizing materials for thematic units in a variety of areas
- Use of systematic lesson planning emphasizing long and short-term goals and assessment
- Implementation of positive classroom management strategies
- Motivation of students through an active learning environment
- Extensive utilization of manipulatives in math and science
- Communication with parents through a weekly newsletter

PRACTICA EXPERIENCE
Kindergarten-intergenerational service learning project, Smith Elementary, Boise, Fall '98
Reading Recovery Program, First Grade, Hope Elementary, Idaho Falls, Summer '98
HACAP Head Start Community Center-basic developmental reading skills, Idaho Falls, Spring '97
Third Grade-skills development in reading and writing, Lakeview Elementary, Boise, Fall '97

RELATED ACTIVITIES
Idaho Association for the Education of Young Children Child Abuse Identification Training
American Heart Association CPR Certification Pediatrics Volunteer, General Hospital

ATHLETIC EXPERIENCES
ISU All-Conference Soccer Selection MVP Soccer Award-ISU
Coach, ISU Summer Soccer Camps Soccer Coach, under 10 coed
Medallion Award, ISU Athletic Department Certified soccer referee

RACHEL BRAVEHEART
221 College Street
Any City, State 12345
(101) 555-1111

DEGREES

B.A. Elementary Education, University of Nebraska - Lincoln   June 1999
Area of Specialization: Language Arts   Minor: Native American Studies
A.A. Liberal Arts, Nebraska Indian Community College, Winnebago, Nebraska   1992

INTERNSHIP EXPERIENCE

Fifth and Sixth Grade Combination Classroom, American Horse Day School, Allen, South Dakota, January - May 1999.

Sixth Grade Language Arts Classroom, Ogallala Middle School Summer Enrichment Program, Ogallala, Nebraska, Summer 1998.

Fourth Grade Open-space Classroom, Field Club Elementary School, Omaha Public Schools, Omaha, Nebraska, Fall 1997.

Teaching highlights included:

Designed curriculum materials that reflect a student-centered approach with many hands-on activities.

Incorporated cross-curricular components into lessons and units. Designed, planned and presented in-depth units on cities, money, measurement, and Native American customs.

Managed three reading groups using both basal materials and literature-based novel units.

Used actual experiences and authentic audiences when teaching reading.

Developed an integrated theme on Plants and Seeds, which infused all subject areas with a literature-based approach.

Taught math and bridged the concrete to the abstract through the use of manipulatives and computer activities.

UNIVERSITY UNDERGRADUATE ASSISTANTSHIP

Research Assistant, Young Reader's Book Program, University of Nebraska - Lincoln, Curriculum and Instruction Division, 1997–1998. Responsible for reading and reviewing new adolescent books. Prepared bibliographies of the materials for use by teachers and curriculum supervisors in Nebraska.

RELATED WORK EXPERIENCE

House Parent, St. Joseph's Indian School, Chamberlain, South Dakota, 1992–1996.
Responsibilities included the care of 12 children in the Family Living Unit. Provided both social and life skills training while meeting the physical, spiritual, and emotional needs of the Sioux Indian children. Also assisted with the planning of the summer program. Program included community activities, summer recreation projects and coaching of the swim team.

Data Entry Clerk and Supervisor, Bureau of Indian Affairs, Pierre Area Office, Pierre, South Dakota, 1987–1989. Maintained records of 58 tribally operated schools in a three-state area. Recorded statistics on the number of students enrolled in public schools and reservation areas. Responsible for updating financial support records from the Bureau of Indian Affairs.

References provided upon request.

COO E. LIGHTFOOT

221 College Street   Any City, State 12345   (101) 555-0009

OBJECTIVE

Teacher: Multiage, Multilevel Elementary Education (K-8)

SPECIAL SKILLS AND INTERESTS

Collaborative Planning	Cooperative Learning
Proactive Classroom Management	Team Teaching
Community Service Emphasis	Individualized Learning
Thematic Approach to Lesson Design	Inclusion
Multicultural Awareness and Teaching Style	Technology Integration

ACADEMIC BACKGROUND

Bachelor of Arts Degree, *with honors* University of North Carolina-Chapel Hill, December 1999

Major: Elementary Education; Area of Specialization: English/Language Arts and Technology

COURSE HIGHLIGHTS

Manual Communication	Literature for Children	Creative Drama in Classroom
Microcomputers for Teachers	Linguistics	Classroom Management
Adolescent Literature	Exceptional Learner	Computer Programming

STUDENT TEACHING EXPERIENCE

Multilevel grades, West Middle School, Big Horn District 121, Horizon, Idaho, Fall Semester 1999 Work in a collaborative setting with a team of six multilevel teachers in a rural school with 175 students of varied abilities, ages 4 to 13 years. Responsibilities include initiating, planning, and implementing service learning projects; integrating reading and writing, grammar, phonics, and spelling into a holistic and individualized curriculum; coordinating and teaching math lessons and activities; observing all subject areas and various teaching techniques; organization of homeroom and beginning-of-day activities for all students; planning, preparing, and organizing materials for thematic units used by various age groups; enhancing and increasing the use of computer technology in the class; and introducing student-led conferences and facilitating student portfolio development.

PRACTICA EXPERIENCE

3rd grade, all subjects including math, science, spelling and language arts, Elk Elementary, Fall 1999
4th-6th grade, community service project-environment and pollution, Hills Elementary, Summer 1999
Multiage, multimedia (computer basics, Internet, CD-ROMs, videodisc) Elk Elementary, Fall 1998
lst grade, reading tutor for at-risk students using integrated approach, Hills Elementary, Spring 1998

References available upon request.

NATALYA WILD-CATT

221 College Street • Any City, State 12345 • (101) 555-0009 • nnoriss@ug.edu

SKILLS
- Emphasis in early reading and language skills
- Experience in direct and indirect instruction for emergent and developing readers
- Training in cooperative learning, writing, storytelling, brain growth, and problem solving

EDUCATION
University of Georgia, Athens, Georgia, B.S. Degree - May, 1999
Majors in Elementary Education and Reading *Honors Commendation*

COURSE HIGHLIGHTS

Literature for Children	Early Literacy Development
Language and Society	Language Processing
Manual Communication	Cognitive Development

READING INTERNSHIP
Reading Clinic, Multiage Class, Lincoln Elementary, Athens, 2/99-4/99
Responsibilities:
- Developed, administered, and scored an Individualized Reading Inventory and Standardized Reading Inventory
- Made individual instructional assessments under guidance of mentor teacher
- Assisted developing readers by using guided reading instruction including conferences and journaling activities
- Used reader's workshop strategies for developing readers using trade books and individual conferences
- Designed and maintained progress charts and conducted case studies
- Communicated with parents on a regular basis
- Attended Child Study team meetings and staffing for learning disabled

STUDENT TEACHING
4th and 5th grades, Salmon Elementary, Athens Public Schools, Fall 1998
Responsibilities:
- Collaborated with teaching teams in social studies, language arts, and math
- Organized and created learning centers stressing technology applications
- Assisted students in developing Hyperstudio presentations and taught QuickTake camera use for student computer demonstrations
- Provided one-on-one tutorial assistance in math help-sessions

RELATED ACTIVITIES
Private tutor, reading/math, Athens Summer Academy, 1999
Hospital pediatrics volunteer, University Hospitals, 1998-1999
Member, Athens Area Reading Council

Credentials at Educational Placement Office, Any City, State 12345 (101) 555-0008
View my Web Site at www.nnn/reading.htm

K.K. YAN

221 College Street   Any City, State 12345   (101) 555-0009

OBJECTIVE	Elementary General Music (K-6)
SPECIALIZED SKILLS	Training in Orff-Schulwerk and Kodaly methods Music technology; synthesizer and audio technology Multicultural experiences Composer and creative producer
INTERNSHIP EXPERIENCE	Elementary General Music and Elementary Instrumental and Strings Tacoma Public Schools, Tacoma, Washington, September 1999 - May 2000 - Taught students in grades K-6 in general and instrumental music classes - Used numerous strategies to motivate students to learn about and appreciate music from various cultural and ethnic backgrounds - Incorporated the use of keyboards, piano, and guitar into classroom - Used Orff and Kodaly teaching techniques with all ages - Served as a guest intern on school district committees including Curriculum Development - K-3 Music, and Computer Applications for K-6
EDUCATION	Pacific Lutheran University, Bachelor of Music Degree - August 2000 Major: Music Education Emphasis: Trumpet Semester exchange program in Beijing, China, 1997
UNIVERSITY ACTIVITIES	Elected President, Student Association-Music Educators Council, 1999-2000 Teaching Assistant, Music Education, Seattle Pacific University, 1999 Received Student Educator-of-the Year Award, Bay Association, 1999 Wrote and directed two musicals for youth, 1998 and 1999 Published: "Electronics in the Elementary Classroom," *Music Educator's Journal,* Vol 12, pp 28-32, 1998 Performer, Seattle Brass Choir (performed in Austria, Italy, and U.S. cities)
AFFILIATIONS	Music Educators National Conference; Northwest Music Educators Music Educators Association; National Education Association
HONORS	Outstanding Performer Award, Pacific Lutheran University Ken March Award for Talented Music Major, Pacific Lutheran University First Chair, Pacific Lutheran University Concert Band Composition Award and Dean's Recognition Award
RELATED EXPERIENCE	Instructor, Summer School, Pacific Music Institute, Seattle, 1999 Supervisor, Chamber Music at Snowmass, Colorado, Summer 1998 Dorm Assistant, Killington Music Festival, Rutland, Vermont, Summer 1997

Credentials at Career Development Office, Any City, State 12345 (101) 555-0008
Portfolio including video and audio available for review

LEE TELDOSI

221 College Street   Any City, State 12345   (101) 555-0008   teldosi@Alcorn.edu

TEACHING INTERESTS

Elementary physical education
- knowledge of child development
- ability to adapt curriculum to students' interests, capabilities, and learning styles
- training in current trends in the field of elementary P.E. curriculum and instructional techniques

EDUCATION

B.S. Degree, May 2000, Mississippi State University, Mississippi State, Mississippi
Major: Physical Education and Leisure Studies   Minor: Psychology and Speech

FIELD EXPERIENCES

Student Teaching: K-5 Physical Education, Oktibbetia County Schools, Fall 1999
Practica: Early Childhood Center, Spring 1999; Jones Middle School, Fall 1998
- Worked in diverse settings as a collaborative team member
- Planned and taught lessons that were appropriate for the growth and development of primary and intermediate age children
- Created various units for different ages including: K-6 parachute unit, early childhood manipulatives unit, K-2 rhythms unit, and a 6-7 track and field unit.
- Stressed cooperative learning, fitness, and lifelong leisure activities in unit plans
- Communicated curriculum and student's progress to parents on a regular basis

SERVICE AND LEADERSHIP

Volunteer coach, elementary track and field clinics, Mississippi State YMCA, 1999
Volunteer, Special Olympics Festival, Southeastern Alliance, Inc., 1999
Member, Intercollegiate Sports Council, Mississippi State University, 1999
Student Representative, Athletics, Mississippi State University, 1997
Letter winner, Mississippi State track and field team, 4 years

CREDENTIALS

Credentials at Career Development Office, Any City, State 12345 (101) 555-0008
Visit my web site at: www.teldosi.edu

LYLE PERMANN

Present address:
221 College Street
Any City, State 12345
(101) 555-1111
email:-permann@nmontana.edu

Permanent address:
30 Royal Avenue
Mytown, State 23456
(909) 333-0003

ACADEMIC TRAINING

M.A., Reading, Northern Montana College, Havre, Montana, June 1999
Thesis: Self-esteem and reading ability in first-grade students
Adviser: Dr. Will B. Proff, Chair, Elementary Education
B.A., Elementary Education (developmental reading emphasis), May 1997

GRADUATE COURSES OF INTEREST

Building Foundations for Reading
Developmental Reading Skills
Seminar: Research and Current Issues

Diagnostic and Prescriptive Approaches
Advanced Reading Clinic Techniques
Brain Growth and Language Ability

CLASSROOM EXPERIENCE

Graduate Internship: Elementary Reading, grades 1-3, School #211, Havre, Montana, Spring 1999. Under supervision of a master reading clinician, used the Reading Recovery Model for individual students in the morning and taught in a reading resource room each afternoon. Utilized five basic instructional activities: (1) rereading a familiar book; (2) reading a new book; (3) mini-lessons; (4) writing/editing; (5) introducing a new book. Carefully assessed students' abilities, evaluated progress, and communicated regularly with parents and classroom teachers.

Reading Practicum: ESL Classroom, Rocky Boy School, Box Elder, Montana, Spring 1998 Taught reading to eleven-year-old students (one from Nigeria, the other from Argentina) in an English as a Second Language classroom. Used a variety of methods to reach students reading at first-grade level. Organized basal, word attack, and language experience units.

Student Teacher: Elementary Basic Skills, Gildford School, Gildford, Montana, Fall 1995 Primary teaching focus was teaching reading and writing in a rural K-8 school with an enrollment of 16 students. Reading focused on comprehension, fluency, word identification, and sight vocabulary. Motivated older students to choose book topics, then rehearsed, drafted, shared, revised, edited, and published individual book reports to be placed in school library.

AFFILIATIONS, HONORS, ACTIVITIES

International Reading Association
Reed A. Lott Scholarship, 1997
Montana State Reading Association

Dean's Achievement Award
Member, Pi Lambda Theta
Greater Montana Area Reading Council

Arts Writer, *The Daily Collegian* newspaper, Northern Montana College, 1998-present
Volunteer Campus Tour Guide, Alumni Association, Northern Montana College, 1996-1998

References provided upon request.

ROSA PEREZ

221 College Street, Any City, State 12345   (101) 555-0007

TEACHING INTERESTS AND SKILLS

Bilingual Early Childhood Special Education
- Develop Individual Education Plans, goals, and program objectives
- Design learning activities that correspond to IEP goals
- Implement effective behavior management strategies for each student
- Work effectively with Spanish-speaking children and parents

STUDENT TEACHING INTERNSHIP

Early Childhood Special Education, Pilot Mountain, North Carolina, Fall 1999
Taught eight students in a rural cooperative program. Duties included:
>Planned and implemented learning activities for students with varied abilities
>Created numerous learning activities that corresponded to IEP goals
>Organized home instruction and incorporated skills across all developmental domains
>Developed with parents and staff appropriate behavior management strategies
>Communicated with children and parents in Spanish

Early Childhood Practicum, Peace Preschool of Raleigh, North Carolina, Fall 1998
Taught pre-kindergarten students in a private setting.
>Developed units in drama, art activities, and beginning reading
>Assisted with preschool screenings in conjunction with local education professionals
>Planned developmentally appropriate activities for various learning centers

Preschool Special Education Practicum, Wake Schools, Raleigh, North Carolina, Spring 1998
Taught four students ages two to four years old in a county program.
>Worked with students in all skill areas and observed mentor teacher work with parents
>Assessed students' strengths and designed and implemented a program for each child

ACADEMIC PREPARATION

Meredith College   May 1999   B.A.   Special Education
Raleigh, North Carolina   Early Childhood

American School of Torréon   1992   Diploma
Torréon, Mexico

RELATED EMPLOYMENT

Preschool Teacher, Centro para Niños, Torréon, Mexico, 1992-1995
Taught in a state-operated child care center where Spanish was the primary language.
>Worked closely with parents to provide appropriate health care and follow-up.

References available upon request

PAUL FLANAGAN
221 College Street
Any City, State 12345
(101) 555-0009

EDUCATION

B.S. - Special Education - Elementary Hearing Impaired
Cleveland State University, Cleveland, Ohio, 1995-1999

Deaf Interpreter Training
Gallaudet University, Washington, D.C., Summer 1999-present

RELATED EXPERIENCE

Student Teaching
Alexander Graham Bell School, Cleveland, Ohio, January - May 1999
Planned and presented lessons in reading, language arts, and mathematics to students ranging from seven to ten years of age. Ungraded curriculum emphasized total communication through an aural-oral approach. With cooperating teacher and other team members, participated in parent conferences and home visits. Observed and assisted with new student entrance and placement tests.

Practicum Experience
Alexander Graham Bell School, September - December 1998
Assisted with skills development in reading and mathematics. Provided individualized instruction in manual communication and finger spelling. Assisted in parent-infant program for children to age 3.

RELATED ACTIVITIES

Camp Counselor, Camp for the Deaf, Nanjemoy, Maryland, Summers 1996-1998
Supervised six campers including deaf boys and their hearing brothers. Taught archery and volleyball skills; assisted with other activities including biking and basketball.

Interpreter, Fairview General Hospital, Cleveland, Ohio, 1995-1999
Volunteer interpreter for hearing-impaired patients or relatives to facilitate communication with hospital staff. Interpreting assignments arranged through the Department of Speech Pathology and Audiology, Cleveland State University.

MEMBERSHIPS

Alexander Graham Bell Association for the Deaf
Convention of American Instructors of the Deaf
Student Member, Ohio Education Association
Phi Kappa Alpha Fraternity

CREDENTIALS
Career Services Center, Any City, State 12345   Telephone: (101) 555-0008

HEATHER BRON

221 College Street
Any City, State 12345
(101) 555-0009 (home)

TEACHING INTERESTS AND SKILLS
- •Teaching severe behavior disabled students in a multidisciplinary team approach
- •Training in behavior management including aversive therapy and alternative discipline plans
- •Experience in support plans addressing consequences and proactive intervention strategies
- •Communicate students' needs to classroom teachers and parents on a regular basis

ACADEMIC BACKGROUND:
> Wagner College, Staten Island, New York
> > Bachelor of Science Degree, Special Education, 1996-2000
> Universidad Granada, Granada, Spain
> > Spanish Language and Literature, 1997

> Licensure: K-6 Special Education, Mild and Moderate Disabilities, State of New York

TEACHING INTERNSHIP EXPERIENCE:
> Wright School, Brooklyn Borough District 18, Brooklyn, New York, Fall 1999
> > •Mental Disabilities, Primary Unit
> > Taught twelve students, ages six to eight, with varied mental disabilities.
> > Worked with students in all skill areas; main emphasis was on concept
> > development, language, and motor and self-help skills. Organized students
> > in instructional groups; worked effectively with the child study team.
> > Attended weekly staff meetings, participated in parent conferences and
> > initiated special parent newsletter.

PRACTICA EXPERIENCE:
> University Hospital School, Brooklyn, New York, 1998
> > Individual work with a twelve-year-old autistic child.
> Rosa Parks Elementary, Summer School Program, Harlem, New York, 1998
> > Taught fifth-grade students with limited English skills.
> Fifth Street Developmental Center, Brooklyn, New York, 1997
> > Assisted severely handicapped students with communication skills.

COLLEGE DISTINCTIONS AND MEMBERSHIPS:
> President-elect, International Student Club   A. Z. Zolinsky Memorial Award Scholarship
> Student Advisory Committee   Member, Council for Exceptional Children

VOLUNTEER AND RELATED WORK EXPERIENCE:
> Behavior Disorders Teacher Associate, Brooklyn Opportunity School, Summer 1999
> Spanish Interpreter, St. Pius Hospital Emergency Room, 1998-present (weekends)
> Volunteer, Special Olympics Track Festival, Staten Island, 1996-1998

REFERENCES AVAILABLE UPON REQUEST FROM
Placement and Teacher Certification
Any City, State 12345 (101) 555-0008 FAX: (101) 555-1118

GRETCHEN T. GRANT
221 College Street
Any City, State 12345
(101) 555-0009

OBJECTIVE
K-12 Substitute Teacher

EDUCATION
University of Texas at Dallas, Richardson, Texas, M.A. Degree - 9/99-present
B.A. Degree - 5/99
Majors: English and Elementary Education   Specialization: Middle School

COURSE HIGHLIGHTS

Exceptional Persons

Classroom Computer Usage

Classroom Management

Teacher-Parent Communication

Methods in Bilingual Education

Special Education Issues

EXPERIENCE

- Student Teacher, Wilson Middle School, Dallas, Texas, Fall 1999
  Responsibilities included teaching various units in sixth, seventh, and eighth grades.
  Participated in a five-member multidisciplinary team including support staff.
  Worked with a diverse population representing more than twenty different countries.

- Writing Tutor, Wilken Elementary, Richardson, Texas, Summer 1998
  Responsibilities included working in the writing lab with attention deficit disorder
  students. Maintained progress reports and communicated regularly with parents.

- Practicum Student, South High School, Dallas, Texas, Spring 1997
  Observed and assisted in ninth-grade general English classes.

- Composition Evaluator, Macmillan/McGraw-Hill, Houston, Summers 1997-present
  Evaluate eighth-grade compositions for the Indiana State Testing of Education Progress.

RELATED ACTIVITIES
Volunteer for Youth Support Services and Pen Pal Partner Program, Summers 1995-1997
Asian Community Center Volunteer and tutor for non-English-speaking adults, 1995-present
Member, National Council of Teachers of English; National Association for Young Children

CREDENTIALS
Career Planning and Placement Center, Any City, State 12345
Telephone: (101) 555-0008

SCOTT HARRIS
221 College Street Any City, State 12345
(101) 555-0009

OBJECTIVE

Teacher: Secondary Agriculture Education

EDUCATION

B.S. Degree, Purdue University, West Lafayette, Indiana, May 1999
  Major: Agriculture Education
  Teaching Certificate, Grades 7-12, May 1999
A.A. Degree, Indiana Vocational Technical College-Lafayette
  Major: Agricultural Technologies - 1994

STUDENT TEACHING

Agriculture Education, South Putnam H.S., Greencastle, Fall 1999
Responsibilities:
- Developed and taught units on soil analysis and farm management
- Team taught two-week ecology unit with biology teacher
- Assisted sponsor of Future Farmers of America with planning and supervision of club activities and fund-raisers
- Graded FFA Proficiency Applications

RELATED EMPLOYMENT

Field research assistant, King Hybrid Seed Company
  Vincennes, Indiana. Summers 1998, 1999

Research assistant, College of Agriculture, Purdue University, 1998
  Tested and analyzed new soybean varieties for use in wet climates.

ACTIVITIES AND AWARDS

- Judged FFA Leadership Contests
- Scholarship, Future Farmers of America
- Dean's List, 5 semesters

MEMBERSHIPS

- Student Member, Indiana Vocational Agriculture Teachers Association
  Secretary, Purdue Chapter, 1998; Program Planning Committee, 1999
- National Vocational Agriculture Teachers Association
- 4-H Member, 10 years; Officer, 4 years

CREDENTIALS ON FILE

Office of Educational Placement
Any City, State 12345 (101) 555-0008

BRAD EMILIA

221 College Street, Any City, State 12345 (101) 555-0009
brad-emilia@sfsuniv.edu   www.brad/bay.htm

TEACHING INTERESTS AND STRENGTHS

Alternative High School Instructor
> Academic strengths in English, History, Math, and Psychology
> Student-Centered Approach with Emphasis on Goal-Setting
> Strong Collaborative Skills

INTERNSHIP EXPERIENCE

San Francisco East Alternative Center, September 1999 to December 1999
> - Worked in a diverse urban school alternative setting that fostered enthusiasm for learning by encouraging student participation and creativity.
> - Involved students in goal-setting, course and career planning.
> - Used innovative methods and materials to produce effective learning experiences that built student pride and increased self-worth.
> - Developed, with mentor teachers, new course syllabi and materials in Fine Arts.
> - Encouraged students to take responsibility for own learning experiences.

PRACTICA EXPERIENCE

At-Risk and Community Liaison, S.E. Junior High School, Oakland, Spring 1999
> - Counseled and worked closely with students who are failing or have extensive absences due to home situations, jobs, or poor study habits and lack of basic skills.
> - Communicate with parents/guardians, parole officers, and social agencies regularly.
> - Maintain careful records and document activities and academic progress.

DEGREES

M.A.   Secondary Education, concentration in Alternative Education, December 1999
San Francisco State University, San Francisco, California

B.A.   History and Psychology Majors, English and Math Minors, July 1997
Stanford University, Stanford, California

PART-TIME EMPLOYMENT AND INTERESTS

Web page developer and computer programmer, Bay Electronics, 1996-present
Piano and bass teacher, private instruction, San Francisco Bay Area, 1995-present
Acoustical and electric bass performer and manager of Bay Jazz
Piano; composing music; playing baseball and working at youth camps

References available at Teacher Career Center, Any City, State 12345 (101) 555-0008

AMANDA JONES - RAYE

221 College Street, Any City, State 12345 (101) 555-0008

TEACHING OBJECTIVE
Art teacher, grades 7-12

EDUCATION
Bachelor of Fine Arts; Studio Emphasis: Printmaking
Duquesne University, Pittsburgh, Pennsylvania, May 1999
Dean's List   Art Education Scholarship

TEACHING EXPERIENCE - Pittsburgh Public Schools
- High School Art: Student teacher, Hoover High School, Fall 1999
  Prepared educational objectives and lesson plans for painting, drawing, sculpture, and jewelry courses at Hoover High School. Assisted with teaching responsibilities in photography.
  Organized student exhibits at the school and the city art museum.
  Submitted student work for consideration in the Pittsburgh Young Artist's Review.
  Attended faculty meetings, participated in school improvement team meetings, volunteered at school functions, and worked with students participating in service-learning activities.

- Middle School Art: Student teacher, E. J. Parks Middle School Center, Spring 1998
  Taught art at three different centers. Created units in bookmaking, metals, multimedia, pottery, fabric design, and multicultural units on Egypt and Mexico.
  Exhibited student artwork in library, display cases, hallways, and classrooms.
  Offered before-school art sessions for enrichment.
  Involved in interdisciplinary team-teaching.

RELATED ART EXPERIENCE
Saturday Morning Art Workshop, Duquesne University, Fall 1998
Volunteer Art Tutor, Eastside Youth Project, Pittsburgh, 1996-1998
High School Painting Workshop, Pittsburgh Alternative Center, 1997
Artist in Residence, North High School, Philadelphia Public Schools, 1997

PROFESSIONAL ORGANIZATIONS
National Art Education Association   Hand Weavers Guild of America
Women's Caucus for Art   National Education Association

CREDENTIALS ON FILE
Career Planning & Placement Center
Any City, State 12345 Telephone: (101) 555-0008

VERONICA A. JOBBE

221 College Street   Any Place, State 12345   (101) 555-0009
                                                                                   jobbe@umiami.edu

Teaching Interests and Skills
- Familiar with 4X4 and A/B Block Scheduling and working in interdisciplinary settings
- Collaborate with colleagues, parents, administrators, support staff, and area scientists
- Academic training in Biology, Physical Science, Environmental Science, Math

Block Scheduling Experience
Junior High Math and Biology, Community School # 22, Miami Public Schools, Fall 1999
High School Science, grades 9 - 12, Block Schedule Program, Fall 1999
- Working in a high school setting implementing a 4X4 block scheduling program; develop lessons to fit block scheduling—four semester-long 90-minute classes per day. Incorporating a variety of teaching strategies including cooperative learning and hands-on approaches to science and math. Work closely with team members in designing course descriptions and information packets for parents and other interested community members.

- Conducted practicum in junior high setting using A/B Block Scheduling. Students enroll for eight 80-minute classes that meet every other day. Effectively used a variety of assessments and motivated students through an active learning environment.

Field Experiences
- Spring 1999: Student taught in a science and mathematics magnet school teaching Biology, Research Lab, and Chemistry. Invited area scientists to present special lab sessions.
- Fall 1998: Participated in an elementary practicum, working in a kindergarten class 6 hours a week for several months. Worked on designing learning centers for science exploration.

Education
University of Miami, Coral Gables, Masters of Arts in Teaching, 1998-present
B.S. Degree, Microbiology, *with honors,* 1993

Professional Organizations
National Science Teachers Association   National Association of Biology Teachers

Research Experience
- Research Assistant II, State of North Carolina Health Center, 1993-1997
Performed laboratory research in a Microbiology lab studying the splicing of RNA in Rous Sarcoma viruses. Presented research (with team members) at regional and national conferences. Co-authored several articles in research journals and newsletters.

Community Service
Volunteer and co-chair, Environmental Preservation Committee for South Florida, 1998 -
Fundraiser, United Way of South Florida   Builder, Habitat for Humanity

---

References available upon request

KELLY McCABE
221 College Street
Any City, State 12345
(101) 555-0009

Teaching Interests

HIGH SCHOOL BUSINESS EDUCATION

Keyboarding	Word Processing	Business Office Machines
Desktop Publishing	Spreadsheets	Consumer Mathematics

Education

Walla Walla College, College Place, Washington, Bachelor's Degree, 1999
        Major: Business Education   Minor: Mathematics

Student Teaching Experience

Business Education, Waitsburg High School, Waitsburg, Washington, Spring 1999

Taught courses in personal computer applications and keyboarding.
Observed and assisted with basic and advanced word processing courses.
Worked with students of diverse backgrounds and varying degrees of experience
    with computer applications, individually and in small and large groups.
Arranged (with supervision from cooperating teacher) for a class visit to a
    regional office technology fair in Spokane, Washington.
Assisted with layout of student newspaper, using PCL and PostScript.
Participated in mid-semester parent conferences.
Co-sponsored student-initiated recycling project.

Practicum Experience

Computer Applications, Walla Walla High School, Spring 1998

Consumer Mathematics, Garrison Junior High School, Spring 1998

Office Technology, Walla Walla High School, Fall 1997

Related Employment

Publications Clerk (work-study position), Public Relations, Walla Walla College, 1997-1998

Assist with word processing for publications including news releases, and page layout for
recruitment brochures and admissions information using PageMaker.

Current Activities and Affiliations

Secretary, Walla Walla College chapter, Student Business Educators' Association
Student representative, faculty search committee
Student Member, Washington State Education Association
Volunteer, Walla Walla County Wildlife Society

Credentials

Office of Career Planning
Any City, State 12345 (101) 555-0008

MARTY PARROTT

221 College Street
Any City, State 12345
(101) 555-0009
marty-parrott@olaf.edu

OBJECTIVE AND SKILLS

English and Language Arts Instructor
- Academic training in Literature (traditional and contemporary) and Writing (creative, poetry, memoir, fiction, and nonfiction)
- Focus on critical reading and continuing literacy beyond the classroom
- Collaboration with teaching teams, administration, and parent groups
- Infuse technology into the classroom via computer writing labs, specialized software, and Internet applications

DEGREE

Bachelor of Arts , English Literature, May, 2000, St. Olaf College, Northfield, MN
graduated with highest distinction   *awarded the President's Medallion*

STUDENT TEACHING

English, Jefferson High School, Minneapolis Public Schools, Fall 1999
Theater, ages 12-18, Loon Acting Academy, Northern Lakes, Summer 1999

Responsibilities included preparation of objectives and lesson plans for three grade levels in a collaborative setting. Extensive instruction in writing strategies and techniques in all classes. Taught 10th-grade American Literature and Language class and several theater courses. Worked closely with students in acting classes and performances. Supervised the computer writing lab and initiated special study review sessions.

SPEECH AND DRAMA

Volunteer Speech Assistant, Northfield High School, 1997-1998
Assisted with play productions and coached members of the speech team involved in interpretation events. Traveled to meets and supervised students.

8th-grade Speech Practicum, Jones Junior High School, 1996
Worked with three sections of students in an elective speech class. Led small group discussions and worked with students on an individual basis.

RELATED ACTIVITIES

Actor, Loon Players Repertory Company and Northfield Community Theatre
Member and stagehand, Northern Lights Center for the Arts, 3 years
Cashier and stocker, College Book & Supply, 2 years
Library Clerk, St. Olaf College Library, 3 years
(Financed schooling through part-time employment and loans)

PROFESSIONAL AFFILIATIONS

Minnesota Communication Association   Speech Communication Association
National Council of Teachers of English   Northfield Teachers Acting Guild

References and portfolio available upon request.

CHELSEA ROBBINS

221 College Street
Any City, State 12345
(101) 555-0009

OBJECTIVE
Teacher - English as a Second Language

ACADEMIC TRAINING

Advanced Studies - Linguistics, University of the South, Sewanee, Tennessee, 1998–1999

B.A. - German, Japanese minor, Miami University, Miami, Ohio, 1993–1997

LANGUAGE BACKGROUND

German:	36 semester hours at Miami University Participated in a six-month advanced language program in Austria Four years of German in high school AFS Student to Karlstadt, Germany, junior year of high school
Japanese:	24 semester hours in Japanese language and culture Worked extensively with a Japanese tutor to enhance speaking skills Traveled to Japan, Summer 1996
Travel and Study Abroad:	Extensive travel in Europe and Japan on four different occasions • Studied at the Regents Summer Program in Austria, 1995 • Intensive language study in St. Radegund • Advanced language study, University of Vienna Hochschulekurs
Other Language Experience:	Resided for three years in the Miami Foreign Language Residence Hall • Involved in various intercultural exchanges with foreign students from Japan, Germany, China, Nepal, Brazil, France, Syria, and other countries • Participated in campus presentations and public intercultural activities • Shared experiences and language study with other students who have lived abroad or traveled extensively

TEACHING EXPERIENCE

Student Teaching:	Stowe Senior High School, Sewanee, Tennessee, and Wells Elementary School, Winchester, Tennessee, Spring 1999 English language assessment and instruction for children with limited or no English language skills from fifteen different countries
Practicum:	Burford Intermediate School, Chattanooga, Tennessee, Fall 1998 Assisted with instruction of two classes of Introductory German, grade 6, and two classes of 7th-grade German. Worked with students individually and in small groups.
Language Lab Attendant:	University of the South, 1998–present Assisted users with language lab technology, answered questions, provided students with resources to complete assignments, and monitored lab equipment.

Credentials available from Career Planning and Placement Center
Any City, State 12345 Telephone: (101) 555-0008

VICTORIA QUEENES

221 College Street
Any City, State 12345
(101) 555-0009

TEACHING COMPETENCIES:

Home Economics	**Health**	**Sponsor**
Life Skills	Substance Abuse	Medical Sciences Club
Interior Design	Disease Prevention	International Students Club
Career Education	Consumer Health	SADD

ACADEMIC TRAINING:

Chicago State University	Bachelor of Science	Majors: Home Economics
Chicago, Illinois	May 1999	Health

STUDENT TEACHING:

Life Skills and Home Economics, Northwest High School, Oak Park Schools, Spring 1999
Responsibilities included teaching units in the following classes:
- Independent Living
- Interior Design
- Family Planning
- Issues in Health
- Worked in a culturally diverse setting with students pursuing vocational career tracks.
  Enriched curriculum with primary resource speakers from community agencies. Worked closely
  with local businesses to establish job-shadowing experiences as well as long-term internships.

PRACTICA EXPERIENCE:

Middle School Health, Sauk Middle School, Barrington, Fall 1998
- Assisted with teaching responsibilities in health; developed a unit on personal health care and sex education
  grades 6-8; led small group activities and organized group follow-up sessions
- Volunteered to supervise after-school study lab and to work with students individually.

Elementary Health, Grant Elementary, Chicago Public Schools, Spring 1998
- Created a multidisciplinary unit on drugs and their consequences
- Invited a doctor to talk to students about addiction and lifelong effects and prevention strategies

OTHER WORK EXPERIENCE:

Tutor - Regional Services for Youth Organization, North ShoreCares, Inc. 1999
Counselor for terminally ill children - Camp Sunbreak, Miami, Summers 1998-1999
Day care provider - Emergency Child Care Services of Chicago, 1997-1998

References available upon request.

J. J. TOPHER

221 College Street, Any City, State 12345 (101) 555-0009
jjtopher@ ubrown.edu

TEACHING SKILLS
Japanese, grades 6-12
English as a Second Language, all levels

DEGREES
M.A. Asian Studies, Brown University, Providence, 1999
    Japanese with Teaching Certification Program
B.A. Major: Linguistics; Minor: East Asian Languages, 1997

INTERNSHIP
Japanese, grades 6-12, Bellton Academy, Providence, Fall 1999
- Taught Japanese on 4 levels including a newly created Honors Class
- Assisted in the coordination of interdisciplinary projects with social
  studies classes and art classrooms
- Integrated technology into daily teaching with specialized
  software, video discs, CD-ROMs, and WWW research
- Developed alternative assessment methods including portfolios

ESL EXPERIENCE
English Teacher, Osaka Schools, Osaka, Japan, 1997-1998
- Team-taught, with Japanese mentor, English in three high schools
- Created daily lesson plans on grammar, spelling, and vocabulary
- Developed numerous supplementary teaching materials to use in
  the classroom and to share with students for nightly review
- Presented seminars and workshops to area teachers and
  participated in several cultural exchange programs

AFFILIATIONS
Rhode Island Second Language Educators
Association of Teachers of Japanese

PART-TIME WORK
Interpreter, Wong Travel Agency, Providence, 1998-present
Tutor, Japanese language, private students, 1998-present
Web page designer, Rhode Island Design Solutions, 1998

REFERENCES
Available upon request.
Visit my Web site at www.topher/esl.htm

JULIA HERMANOS

221 College Street, Any City, State 12345
101-555-0009 (home) 101-555-1111 (business)

OBJECTIVE:
> Journalism teacher and student newspaper advisor.

CURRENT PROFESSIONAL EXPERIENCE:
> Staff Writer, *Daily Times*, Montgomery, Alabama, 2000-
> Cover education and city hall news. Supervise students in the High School Reporting
> Internships Program sponsored by the *Daily Times*.

EDUCATIONAL FIELD EXPERIENCES:
> Student Teacher, Journalism, Montgomery Public Schools, fall semester 1999
> Intern in Journalism classes, Huntsville City Schools, spring semester 1998

> Responsibilities included teaching classes in Foundations of Journalistic
> Writing, Advertising, and Mass Media, and supervising Newsmagazine Lab.
> Taught journalistic writing, design, desktop publishing, editing, and paste-up.
> Assisted students in campaign to increase advertising sales.

GRADUATE COURSE HIGHLIGHTS:

Journalistic Writing and Reporting	Media and the Consumer
Editing Workshop	Legal and Ethical Issues in Communication
Publication Design Workshop	Gender and Mass Communication

ACADEMIC TRAINING:

Master of Arts Degree	School of Journalism and Mass Communication
	Alabama State University, Montgomery, 1999
Bachelor of Science Degree	Journalism Major, Global Studies Minor
	Auburn University, Auburn, Alabama, 1995

PROFESSIONAL ASSOCIATIONS:
> American Society of Journalists and Authors
> Association for Education in Journalism and Mass Communications
> National Association of Hispanic Journalists

PRESENTATIONS:
> "Teaching Students Their Rights as Young Editors," Pre-conference workshop presentation,
> Association for Education in Journalism and Mass Communication,
> New Orleans, Louisiana, August 2000
> "Newspaper Labs in High Schools: Partnerships with Local Newspapers," address at State
> Conference for High School Journalism Teachers, Atlanta, Georgia, May 1999
> Panel Member, "Ethics in Reporting: Whose Ethics?" Investigative Reporters and Editors
> Conference, West Palm Beach, Florida, October 1998

REFERENCES:
> Furnished Upon Request

KIM SOON

221 College Street, Any City, State 12345 (101) 555-0009

TEACHING COMPETENCIES

Advanced Algebra and Calculus   Algebra and Geometry   Statistics and Measurement
General Mathematics   Trigonometry   Computer Programming

Completed Principles of Technology training
Knowledge of national math standards and essential academic learnings
Instructional skills include cooperative learning, questioning strategies, and concept development
Use technology in advanced and basic classes to demonstrate concepts and to teach computer skills

EDUCATION

Teacher Certification Program, Mathematics, August 1999, Marquette University, Milwaukee

Bachelor of Science Degree - Mathematics, 1994-1997, Virginia State University, Chesterfield
- Dean's List   • Presidential Citation   • Hammond Math Scholarship

CLASSROOM TEACHING EXPERIENCE

Internship: Mathematics, Kansas City Public Schools, Kansas City, Kansas, 1/99-5/99
Taught algebra, geometry, and calculus, in an inner-city magnet school, using a variety of teaching and motivational strategies to encourage students to reach their potential. Identified areas of difficulty and prepared lessons to assist students in overcoming them. Incorporated a computer program to increase problem solving and reasoning abilities. Volunteer supervisor of Math Club and Computer Programming Club.

Practicum: Elementary Mathematics, Pine Elementary, Milwaukee, Wisconsin, 10/98-12/98
Taught students of varied abilities in a grade 5/6 combination classroom. Designed special activities to demonstrate math concepts; reinforced learning through computer-assisted instruction. Attended in-service meetings and school events; observed and participated in parent-teacher conferences.

RELATED EXPERIENCE

Tutor in basic computer applications, Milwaukee and Kansas City, 1997-present
Resident Assistant, Pennsylvania Towers, Virginia State University, 1995-1998
Camp Counselor for at-risk 10-12 year olds, Nine Springs, Colorado, Summers 1993-1995

PROFESSIONAL MEMBERSHIPS

Missouri Council of Teachers of Mathematics   National Council of Teachers of Mathematics
National Education Association   Phi Delta Kappa

Credentials on file at Career Services Center, Any City, State 12345 (101) 555-0008

AHMED KHAN
221 College Street
Any City, State 12345
(101) 555-0009

EDUCATION

B.A. - Education - Language Arts and Social Studies Emphasis - 1999
Rhode Island College, Providence, Rhode Island

STUDENT TEACHING

Esek Hopkins Middle School, Providence, Rhode Island, February - June 1999
• Team teaching in integrated Language Arts/Social Studies program, grades 5-6
• Developed writing skills using a "writers workshop" mode of instruction
• Prepared units on history and biographies of the colonial period
• Created bulletin boards and interest centers to emphasize contributions of women
      to colonial social and cultural history
• Practiced effective classroom management techniques to promote student achievement
• Devised projects for individual investigation and small group collaboration suitable
      for students with a wide range of interests and achievement levels
• Assisted with supervision of pupils in out-of-classroom activities
• Participated in grade level curriculum and team meetings
• Attended and participated in parent conferences to discuss student progress and to
      interpret school programs and expectations

PRACTICUM EXPERIENCE

Oliver Hazard Perry Middle School, Providence, Rhode Island, September-October 1998
• Observed and participated in language arts instruction; worked with individual students on
      vocabulary building and improving reading skills; volunteered to assist with layout
      of magazine featuring student prose, poetry, and artwork.
Urban Collaborative Accelerated Program, Providence, Rhode Island, April-May 1998
• Observed team of three teachers employing an integrated approach to language arts and social
      studies instruction with students of exceptional abilities and a wide range of interests;
      observed team planning and evaluation sessions.

RELATED ACTIVITIES

Playground and Cafeteria Monitor, Mary E. Fogarty School, Providence, Rhode Island, 1996-1999
      Supervised lunchroom and playground behavior of elementary students (K-6) to
      ensure and promote safety and consideration for other students.

MEMBERSHIPS

Rhode Island Student Education Association
Institute for Democracy in Education Association
Rhode Island College Society for Creative Anachronism
Volunteer, Student Cooperative Bookstore

CREDENTIALS

Career Development Center
Any City, State 12345
(101) 555-0008

LUCY JASPER

221 College Street, Any City, State 12345 (101) 555-0009
lucy-jasper@uminn.edu

TEACHING INTERESTS	Block Team Member	Mathematics	Science
	Interdisciplinary	Physical Education	Reading

EXTRACURRICULAR INTERESTS
Coaching Softball, Swimming, and Basketball
Sponsoring student clubs and working with community groups

EDUCATION
University of Minnesota-Minneapolis
M.A. Degree, Education, May 1999   *Middle School*
Concentration: mathematics and reading   *Emphasis: science*
B.S. Degree, Exercise Science, May 1997   *with honors*

State Teaching License, Elementary K-6; Middle School 6-8
State Coaching Certificate—all sports

HONORS
Invited Member, Honors Program   Dean's List, 6 semesters
Twin Cities Women's Club Scholarship   Governor's Youth Award, 1994

INTERNSHIP EXPERIENCES
Resource Specialist, Special Semester Intern, St. Paul Schools, 8/99-12/99
Middle School Interdisciplinary Unit Intern, I.E. Magnet School, Fall 1998
Responsibilities of above internship experiences include:
- Planning educational objectives and lesson plans for interdisciplinary units for middle school students with a wide range of ability levels including non-English speakers, special needs, and academically accelerated students
- Use of a wide variety of strategies including cooperative learning, technology integration, with emphasis on goal-setting and student responsibility
- Using positive and proactive classroom management strategies
- Working in a team setting, attending in-services and grade-level meetings
- Conducting parent-teacher conferences and student-led parent conferences

FIELD EXPERIENCE
Science Education, middle school   Math, grade 7
Physical Education, all ages   Language Arts, ages 9 to 13
General Education, ages 8 to 12   Reading, grades 7 and 8

ATHLETIC EXPERIENCE
Summer Umpire, North Havenship Little League, 1998; Softball Coach, 1999
Head Student Athletic Trainer, Softball, University of Minnesota, 1996-1998

REFERENCES
References available upon request; visit my Web site at www.lucy/teacher.htm

JESSE HOLBROOK

221 College Street, Any City, State 12345 (101) 555-1111
j-holbrook@pennst.edu

TEACHING INTERESTS

Middle School language arts; strong background in the writing process including grammar and usage; technology integration emphasis.

DEGREES

The Pennsylvania State University, University Park, Pennsylvania

M.A., English Education, June 1999

Thesis: Assessment of Skills Development in Portfolios of Student Writing

Advisor: Dr. Willa Pruvitt, Department Chair

B.A., English Education, 1996; Emphases: Language Arts and Middle School Education

CLASSROOM EXPERIENCE

Student Teaching Internship - Middle School Language Arts, Hannah Middle School, York, Pennsylvania, October 1998 - May 1999. Taught multiethnic students at all learning levels. Initiated the development of writing portfolios; held regular conferences with individual students. Participated in middle school team approach to teaching; prepared interdisciplinary lessons and units. Also incorporated cooperative learning activities into the curriculum; provided peer tutoring services for students needing additional help.

English 9 Practicum Experience, Elk Lake Junior-Senior High School, Dimock, Pennsylvania, Spring 1997. Taught thematic units on survival, handicaps, and fantasy; incorporated poetry, prose and drama. Established daily journal writing in class. Integrated whole language reading and writing activities within established curriculum.

VOLUNTEER TEACHING EXPERIENCE

Instructor, English as a Second Language. Czech Republic (sponsored by Education for Democracy/U.S.A., Inc.), September 1996 - August 1997. Taught English conversation to grammar school students ages 8-13. Responsible for creating and developing curriculum and teaching materials.

RELATED EXPERIENCE

National Outdoor Leadership School, Lander, Wyoming, Summer 1998

Five-week wilderness and mountaineering expedition. Activities included skills training, leadership development, backpacking, rock climbing, snow and glacier travel.

Herencia Espanola, Madrid University, Madrid, Spain, Summer 1996

Participated in 60 hours of Spanish language and culture classes and a week of travel in Spain with students from more than 30 countries.

References and Portfolio provided upon request.

MARTHA REDWIN
221 College Street
Any City, State 12345
(101) 555-0009

OBJECTIVE	**Middle School Reading Teacher**

EDUCATION
Old Dominion University, Norfolk, Virginia
 B.A. Degree - June 1999 - Major: Reading

Université de Léon, Léon, France
 Year Abroad Program, 1997
 Emphases: Literature and Art

COURSE
HIGHLIGHTS

Methods: High School Reading   Diagnostic Techniques
Literature for Children   Current Issues in Reading
Reading Clinic   Building Foundations for Reading

EXPERIENCE

Teaching Internship:
Middle School Developmental Reading, Norfolk Public Schools, 1/99-6/99
 Major areas of teaching and related activities included:
  •Word identification
  •Sight vocabulary
  •Comprehension
  •Fluency
  •Integrating of reading and writing
  •Self-selected reading

Practica:
High School Reading (9th grade), Metro Alternative Center, Norfolk
 Fall semester 1998
Intermediate Grade Reading, Edison Elementary School, Norfolk
 Spring semester 1998
Advanced Reading for Gifted Students (3rd grade), St. Lukes Academy,
 Summer 1998

Travel and Language Ability:
Fluent in French; lived with a French family, 1997
Traveled extensively in Europe

RELATED
ACTIVITIES

Pen Pal Partner, Norfolk Neighborhood Projects, 1998-1999
Reader for the Blind, Old Dominion Special Services, 1998
Volunteer reader for local senior citizens' center, 1998
International Reading Association, Member

CREDENTIALS   Educational Career Services, Any City, State 12345 (101) 555-0008

PETER WELCHER
221 College Street
Any City, State 12345
(101) 555-0009

OBJECTIVE:	**Middle School Tech Lab Instructor**

DEGREES:

University of Oklahoma, Norman, Oklahoma
    Bachelor of Science Degree - May 2000
        Major: Computer Science

Oklahoma Junior College of Business and Technology, Tulsa, Oklahoma
    Associate Degree - June 1995
        Area: Electronics

FIELD
EXPERIENCES:
(1999)

Student Teacher - Technology Lab, Irving Middle School, Norman, Oklahoma
Practicum Teacher - Computer Lab, Little Axe High School, Norman, Oklahoma
Methods Class - Electronics Class, Senior High School, Norman, Oklahoma

Student teaching responsibilities included:
Teaching computer assisted instruction in a number of tech modules
in a newly established technology lab. Modules included hands-on
applications in electronics, transportation manufacturing, hydraulics,
drafting, robotics, engineering, and audiovisual productions.
Student-centered modules were designed to provide realistic experiences
and career-related information.

WORK
EXPERIENCE:

Electronics Specialist, Oklahoma Light and Power Company, Tulsa, Oklahoma
    1992 - 1996

Electronics Apprentice, Tulsa Lighting Company, Tulsa, Oklahoma
    1990 - 1992

Semi-truck Driver, Monfort Trucking, Denver, Colorado
    1983 - 1985

MILITARY:

U. S. Navy, Electronic Specialist, 1985 - 1989
    Served on the battleships U.S.S. Missouri and Iowa
    Tours included the Pacific Rim and the Persian Gulf area

INTERESTS:

Model airplanes (President of local Model Airplane Association)
Antique Auto Repair
Private Flight Instructor

CREDENTIALS
ON FILE:

Teacher Career Center
Any City, State 12345 (101) 555-0008

Lotte Noyes

221 College Street • Any City, State • 12345
(319) 555-1111 • lotte-noyes@uhawaii.edu

TEACHING INTERESTS

K-12 Instrumental or General Music
- Concert, jazz, marching, and pep bands, ensembles, private and large group instruction.
  - Skills in piano, percussion, guitar, and all band instruments.

ACADEMIC TRAINING

Bachelor of Music Degree, May 1999, University of Hawaii at Manoa
Major: Music Education, K-12 Emphasis: Percussion
Honors: with distinction, Dean's List, Academic and Music Performance Scholarship

STUDENT TEACHING AND PRACTICA EXPERIENCE

High school and elementary instrumental music, Honolulu Public Schools, Fall 1999
Middle school instrumental and elementary general music practica, Spring 1999
Planned and prepared lesson plans emphasizing long- and short-term goals and assessment for all grades. Implemented positive classroom management strategies and encouraged students from diverse backgrounds to participate. Effectively conducted full band and small ensembles; instructed students on all band instruments during individual and group lessons. Participated in large group band contests and solo and ensemble contests, grades 7-12.

RELATED ACTIVITIES

Private music instructor, guitar and piano, 1998-present
All-State Music Camp Instructor & Small Ensemble Director, University of Hawaii, Summers 1998-1999

PERFORMANCE ACCOMPLISHMENTS - UNIVERSITY OF HAWAII

Jazz Band and Jazz Ensembles
Symphonic Orchestra and Band (performances in California, Nevada, New York)
Marching Band (performed at Rose Bowl Parade, Aloha Bowl, Kick-Off Classic)

OTHER WORK EXPERIENCE

Clerk, Pediatric Department, Pacific Hospitals and Clinics, two years
University Computer Lab Assistant, Residence Halls, three years

COMPUTER TECHNOLOGY

SOFTWARE:	Microsoft Word	GENERAL SKILLS:	Web Page Design
	Excel		Databases
	Finale		Desktop Publishing

References and Web site address available upon request.

JULIA M. DALLAS

221 College Street, Any City, State 12345 (101) 555-0009

Teaching Competencies

VOCAL
Concert and Swing Choirs
Vocal Instruction
Choir (7th-12th)
Ensembles

SPECIAL INTERESTS
Contest Entries
All-State Participation
State and Regional Contests
Music Booster Club

Academic Training

University of Alaska-Fairbanks, Teacher Certification in K-12 Music December 1999

Arizona State University - Tempe, Bachelor of Music Degree, 1997, Voice Performance

Student Teaching

H.S. Music, Yukon Flats High School, Beaver, Alaska, Fall 1999
- Taught instrumental and vocal music appreciation classes
- Used elements such as melody, harmony, rhythmic notation, form, and analysis
- Provided tutorial services for students wishing advanced training
- Incorporated cultural songs and special native Alaskan activities into classes
- Evaluated student progress by offering private lessons and small group sessions
- Performed local concerts and participated in regional contests

Practicum Experience

Middle School Vocal Music, Yukon Middle School, Arctic Flats, Spring 1998
- Assisted with teaching responsibilities in general music classes and choir
- Worked with small group music ensembles
- Reviewed music curriculum and related teaching materials

Activities and Awards

University Concert Choir, Arizona State, 4 years; Leading roles in two operas
Performed in numerous musicals, 4 years; Member of Chamber Singers
Arizona State Music Scholarship; Dean's List, 7 semesters; Graduated with distinction

Other Work Experience

All-State music instructor and camp supervisor - Arizona State Summer Camp, 1999
Private music lessons - vocal and violin - Tempe and Fairbanks, Summers 1998-present

Credentials at Teacher Placement Center, Any City, State 12345 (101) 555-0008

NICHOLAS TRESNAK

221 College Street
Any City, State 12345
(101) 555-0009

OBJECTIVE:

Physical Education Instructor, grades K-12
Adaptive Physical Education Instructor, Middle School
Extracurricular interests in coaching men's or women's tennis

EDUCATION:

Iowa State University, Ames, Iowa
Bachelor of Science Degree - May 1999
Major: Exercise Science with emphasis in Physical Education
Minor: Special Education

LICENSURE:

Iowa Professional Teaching License, Physical Education, grades K-12
Adaptive Physical Education Endorsement, grades K-8
State of Iowa Coaching Authorization

TEACHING INTERNSHIPS:

Elementary Physical Education, Edwards Elementary School, Ames, Iowa, 8/98 - 10/98
High School Physical Education, Ames High School, Ames, Iowa, 10/98 - 12/98
Adaptive Physical Education, Nevada Middle School, Nevada, Iowa, 1/99 - 3/99
Responsibilities:
- Taught students at all levels from kindergarten to high school seniors.
- Used various teaching techniques to allow for differing learning styles.
- Worked with adaptive physical education students and developed appropriate skill-level activities.
- Established an active learning environment through positive feedback.
- Assisted with the organization of the Heart Association's Jump Rope for Heart.
- Observed special education classes and met with teachers to better serve adaptive physical education students.
- Participated in coordination of the Fine Arts Festival at Edwards Elementary.

PRACTICA:

Special Education, Ames Middle School, Ames, Iowa, Fall 1997
Adaptive Physical Education, Parkview Middle School, Ankeny, Iowa, Fall 1997
Health Education, Ankeny High School, Ankeny, Iowa, Spring 1996
Physical Education, Ames High School, Ames, Iowa, Fall 1996

COACHING:

Tennis, Club Coach for University Athletic Club, Ames, Iowa, Summers 1997 - present
Tennis, Student Coaching, Ankeny High School, Ankeny, Iowa, Spring 1998
Tennis, Private Coach, Ames and Ankeny areas, 1996 - 1998

AWARDS:

- Dean's List, 1999
- Iowa State tennis team: letter winner - 3 years; MVP - 1 year
- Nominated for the Big Eight Conference Athlete of the Year, 1999
- University Student Award for Volunteer Service, 1999
  (Volunteer service at Mary Greely Hospital, Boys' Juvenile Center, and the United Action for Youth Center)

ACTIVITIES:

Member, American Alliance for Health, Physical Education, Recreation and Dance
Student Delegate, 1998 AAHPERD National Convention
Member, Iowa Alliance for Health, Physical Education, Recreation and Dance

REFERENCES:

Career Development Center, Any City, State 12345 (101) 555-0008

J. L. DVORAK

221 College Street
Any City, State 12345
(101) 555-0009

OBJECTIVE: **Teacher: Russian Language (9-12)**

EDUCATION: The Ohio State University, Columbus, Ohio
B.S. Degree - May 1999
Major: Russian Language
Teaching Certificate, May 1999

The Pushkin Institute, Moscow, Russia
Exchange Program - September 1997 - June 1998

Middlebury College, Middlebury, Vermont
Summer 1997 - Russian Language

Bryn Mawr College, Bryn Mawr, Pennsylvania
Summer 1996 - Russian Language

STUDENT TEACHING: **Russian Language**, Valley High School, Columbus, 1/99-5/99
Responsibilities:
- Prepared lesson plans and objectives for levels I-IV
- Reviewed curriculum resources and created new materials
- Attended departmental meetings and support groups
- Effectively used cooperative learning strategies
- Implemented higher order thinking skills
- Involved in International Club
- Organized and created grammar explanations, games, and activities

PRACTICUM STUDENT: **English as a Second Language**, Art Middle School, Detroit, 9/98-1/99
Responsibilities:
- Assisted in all teaching responsibilities
- Provided tutorial services for students needing extra help
- Individually tutored new students

ACTIVITIES AND AWARDS:
- Dean's List, 1994-1999
- Ohio Critical Language Program, accepted 1996
- Member, American Association of Slavic and Eastern European Languages
- Member, Dobro Slovo, Slavic Honor Society
- Buckeye Marching and Concert Band, 1994-1996
- President, Russian Circle, 1995

CREDENTIALS ON FILE: Teacher Career Center
Any City, State 12345 (101) 555-0008

JOHN SEEMAN

221 College Street Any City, State 12345 (101) 555-0009
jseeman@nwu.edu

COMPETENCIES

SCIENCE
Biology
Earth Science
Environmental Studies

MATH
Algebra
Geometry
Business Math

SPONSOR
Science Club Sponsor
National Honor Society
Math Bee Advisor

COACH
Baseball-Varsity
Pitching Specialist
Summer Youth Programs

DEGREES

Northwestern University, Evanston, Illinois, M.A. Science Education, June 1999
Lake Forest College, Lake Forest, Illinois, B.A. Biology and Mathematics, May 1997
Graduated with highest distinction Dean's List Nat Scholar, 1996

INTERNSHIP EXPERIENCE

H.S. Science, Evanston High School, Fall 1999
• Taught Biology I, Advanced Biology, Environmental Studies and Global Issues
- Provided students the opportunity to use creativity and higher-order thinking skills
- Developed rubrics for student group evaluations and portfolio assessment
- Designed labs for all learners and provided materials for accelerated students

PRACTICUM EXPERIENCE

Math and Science, Lincoln Middle School, Chicago Public Schools, Fall 1998
• Assisted with teaching responsibilities in exploratory science
• Organized and led small group activities in advanced sixth-grade math
• Taught integrated unit with English Department on rain forests and global impact
• Involved in supervising computer lab for seventh-grade math students

AFFILIATIONS

Co-chair, Campus Recycling Committee; Member, Lake Pollution Coalition
Illinois Academy of Science; National Science Teachers Association

ATHLETIC AND RELATED EXPERIENCES

Scholarship Baseball Player, All Conference Pitcher, MVP, Most Inspirational
Math Tutor - University Special Support Services, Northwestern University, 1999
Camp Counselor - Camp Wildcat, Northwestern University, Summers 1998 and 1999

Portfolio and references available upon request.
Visit my Web site: www.seeman/science.htm

JENNIFER KIDWELL

221 College Street
Any City, State 12345
(101) 555-0009

TEACHING STRENGTHS

- World History
- European History

- Government
- Geography

*Will direct or assist in student government,
model UN, debate, and class sponsorship*

ACADEMIC BACKGROUND

History - B.A. *(with distinction)* - 1998
University of Southern Colorado, Pueblo, Colorado

STUDENT TEACHING EXPERIENCE

Poudre School District, Fort Collins, Colorado, Fall 1998
Secondary Social Studies.
Prepared educational objectives and lesson plans for three levels. Worked with individuals, small groups, and large groups using a variety of teaching strategies. Conducted after-school study and tutoring sessions. Student teaching consisted of a full-day, full-semester experience. Worked extensively with the following three classes:

- *Africa and Latin America:* Used simulations, media, guest speakers, and small group activities to familiarize students with issues and problems confronting lesser-developed countries (LDCs). Topics included debt, development, environment, and international relations. Concentrated on verbal and critical thinking skills.

- *World History:* Taught medieval history to remedial students. Developed a major unit on the concept of nation-building. Concentrated on improving students' study skills.

- *European History:* Taught ancient and medieval European history to tenth and eleventh graders. Prepared and taught a unit on castles and serfdom. Concentrated on students' research and writing skills.

RELATED EXPERIENCE

Middle School Social Studies, practicum, Franklin Middle School, Pueblo, Spring 1996
Tutor, Community Center Adult Learning Program, Pueblo, 1995-present
Crisis Center Volunteer, Crisis Center, Pueblo, 1996-present
Big Brother/Big Sister Partner, Pueblo, 1995, 1997

CREDENTIALS

Education Placement Office, Any City, State 12345
Telephone: (101) 555-0008 FAX: (101) 555-0089

TASSIE LONESTAR

221 College Street, Any City, State 12345 (101) 555-0009

TEACHING OBJECTIVE

Spanish: Grammar, Latin American Culture, Spanish Culture, Literature and History
Journalism: News Reporting, Journalistic Writing, Photography, Broadcast Journalism

INTERESTS

Soccer Coaching	Student Government	Yearbook Sponsor
Swimming Instructor	Cheerleading Sponsor	Newspaper Advisor

EDUCATION

Kent State University, Kent, Ohio, Teacher Certification - Spanish, December 1999
Luther College, Decorah, Iowa, B.A. with Double Major - Journalism/Spanish, 1997
International Language Study in Mexico and Spain, 1997 and 1998

STUDENT TEACHING

Spanish, Roosevelt High School, Kent, Ohio, Fall 1999
- Taught Spanish classes on levels I, II, III, and IV
- Utilized effective classroom management techniques
- Provided tutorial services for students needing additional help
- Incorporated special activities and guest speakers into curriculum
- Evaluated student progress and held regular student conferences
- Attended in-service sessions, faculty meetings, and school functions

PRACTICUM STUDENT

Journalism, Revere High School, Richfield, Ohio, Spring 1999
- Assisted with teaching responsibilities in journalism and mass communication
- Organized and led small group activities focusing on ethics in journalism
- Developed and taught a unit on magazine writing and editing
- Supervised newspaper lab using desktop publishing technologies

ACTIVITIES AND AWARDS

Dean's List; All-Conference tennis player and team captain, Luther College
Member, American Council for the Teaching of Foreign Languages
Volunteer cheerleading sponsor, City High School, three years
Summer camp counselor - Camp Foster, Arnolds Park, Iowa, two summers

Credentials at Career Planning & Placement, Any City, State 12345   (101) 555-0008

MARIE LOVETINSKY

221 College Street
Any City, State 12345
(101) 555-0009

OBJECTIVE	**Special Education** instructor at secondary level
DEGREES	**Master of Arts Degree**, Special Education Indiana State University, Terre Haute, Indiana 12/99 **Bachelor of Arts Degree**, Special Education St. Mary's College, Notre Dame, Indiana 5/98
STUDENT TEACHING	**High School Special Education**, Johnson High School, Terre Haute, Indiana 8/99-10/99 **Middle School Special Education**, Horace Mann School, Indianapolis, Indiana 10/99-12/99 *Responsibilities of the above positions included instruction of mild mental disabilities-educable in a special class with integration and moderate mental disabilities- trainable in a special self-contained class. Assessed and evaluated the individual needs of students with learning, mental, and behavior disabilities. Designed and utilized IEP goals and objectives. Organized and implemented lessons in the four curricular domains with the main emphasis on concept development, language, communication, motor and self-help skills. Worked with a special education team consisting of consultant, physical therapist, occupational therapist, and speech therapist.*
PRACTICA	**Adaptive Physical Education Assistant**, South Bend High School, South Bend, 9/96-5/97 **Life Skills Training Assistant**, Regional Services Office, Terre Haute, 6/97-12/97 **Behavior and Emotional Disorders**, North Junior High School, Bloomington, 10/98-12/98
RELATED ACTIVITIES	**Volunteer**, Special Olympics, 4 years **Organizer and volunteer**, Terre Haute Special Populations Support Group **Officer**, College of Education Student Service Organization
PART-TIME EXPERIENCE	<u>Week-end manager</u>, Active Endeavors Sports, Indianapolis, 1996-1999 <u>Clerk</u>, Campus Book & Supply, Terre Haute (part-time), 1998 <u>Receptionist</u>, St. Mary's Admissions Center, 1994-1997 *(Financed college expenses through employment and loans)*
PROFESSIONAL AFFILIATIONS	Indiana State Education Association National Education Association Council for Exceptional Children Pi Lambda Theta Phi Delta Kappa
CREDENTIALS	Career Planning and Placement Center Any City, State 12345-1338 Telephone: (101) 555-0008

JIMMY J. TUO

221 College Street   Any City, State 12345   (101) 555-0009

TEACHING STRENGTHS
- Speech and Drama
- Mass Communication
- Play Production
- Contemporary Literature

will direct play productions, small group and individual drama contest events

STUDENT TEACHING EXPERIENCE

Speech and English Department, Albany School District #1, Laramie, Wyoming, Fall 1999
Student taught an advanced speech course, 10th-grade American Literature & Language course, upperclass Mass Communications and team-taught an elective speech class for juniors. Prepared educational objectives and lesson plans for three grade levels. Worked with individuals, small groups, and large groups using a variety of instructional and motivational strategies. Supervised students in the computer writing lab and initiated special after-school study reviews sessions.

Speech and Drama Volunteer, Albany School District #1, Laramie, 1999 - present
Assisted with play productions and coached members of the speech team involved in interpretation events. Traveled to meets, chaperoned, and supervised students.

Middle School Language Arts, Big Horn Middle School, Big Horn, Wyoming, Fall 1998
Assisted with lesson plans and progress reports. Worked with three language arts classes during novel unit. Led small group discussions and met with students on an individual basis.

RELATED EXPERIENCE
Stage assistant, costume and scenery construction, University of Wyoming Productions
Actor, Wyoming Players Repertory Company (traveling company performing statewide)
Set designer and part-time actor, Big Horn Mountains Community Theatre
Member and weekend supervisor, Gold Usher Corps, Wyoming Arts Center

DEGREES
Bachelor of Arts Degree, August 1999, University of Wyoming, Laramie, Wyoming
graduated with honors

Honors:
Phi Beta Kappa   Dean's List Presidential Citation   Buck Drama Scholarship

Associate of Arts Degree, June 1997, Casper College, Casper, Wyoming
Dean's List

PROFESSIONAL ORGANIZATIONS
Speech Communication Association
National Council of Teachers of English
Wyoming Communication Association
Wyoming Actors Guild

References Available Upon Request
Video Portfolio Available

KEVIN KLADDE
221 College Street
Any City, State 12345
(101) 555-0009

EDUCATION

B.S. Degree - Technology Education - May 2000
University of Wisconsin - Platteville,
Platteville, Wisconsin

TEACHING INTERESTS

Technical Drawing
Architectural Drawing
Construction Technology

Basic Wood Technology
Advanced Wood Technology
Home Maintenance

COACHING INTERESTS

Golf
Track and Field

Assist with:
Baseball, Basketball, Soccer

STUDENT TEACHING

Industrial Technology, Fall 1999, River Valley High School,
Spring Green, Wisconsin
• Planned and presented units on using hand tools and basic carpentry for a
   one-semester Home and Auto Repair course
• Taught drafting exercises including dimensioning, sectional views,
   pictorials, and architectural floor plan design
• Assisted with computer-aided drafting and design
• Worked with individualized and group projects in technical drawing
• On-site supervisor for electrical wiring at student home construction project
• Helped organize annual student project exhibit for all woodworking
   and metal craft classes

RELATED ACTIVITIES

Assistant Track Coach, River Valley High School, Spring 2000
Softball Coach, Platteville Parks Program, 1997-1999
Golf Team, University of Wisconsin-Platteville, 1996-2000

RELATED EMPLOYMENT

Construction Worker, Emerson Developers, Monroe, Wisconsin
Summers 1996-2000

MEMBERSHIPS

Student Member, Wisconsin Industrial Arts Teachers Association
Student Member, Wisconsin Education Association
Corresponding Secretary, local chapter, Wisconsin Antique Auto Club
Citizen Action Network
Sierra Club

CREDENTIALS ON FILE

Teacher Placement Office
Any City, State 12345 (101) 555-0008

VALERIE CIMMINO

221 College Street
Any City, State 12345
(101) 555-0009

EDUCATION

Secondary English - Licensure Program, Urban Teacher Development Project
Paterson Public Schools, Paterson, New Jersey, 1999-2000
The Urban Teacher Development Project awards full scholarships for study and internship opportunities leading to a professional teaching license. The Project is directed by the Paterson Public Schools in collaboration with faculty from teacher preparation institutions throughout the state who teach courses and collaborate with practitioners in the schools to supervise student teaching or internship experiences.

B.A. - Majors in English and Psychology
Glassboro State College, Glassboro, New Jersey, 1993-1997

TEACHING EXPERIENCE

Internship:
Eastside High School, Paterson, New Jersey, January-June 2000
Taught Contemporary Writing and Basic English
Created individual reading plans for each student in Contemporary Writing, an elective course for students in grades 11 and 12 reading at or near grade level. Readings included fiction, essays, and poetry. Emphasized critical reading skills, demonstrated in oral and written responses to readings. In Basic English, required for grade 10, developed units on vocabulary building and expository writing.

Practicum Experience
Eastside and John F. Kennedy High Schools, Paterson, New Jersey, November-December 1999
Observed classes taught by mentors, assisted with presentation of units for individual and group projects in spelling and punctuation. Worked with students individually and in small groups to improve written and oral communication.

RELATED EXPERIENCE

Counselor, Passaic County Family Court, Paterson, New Jersey, 1997-2000
Assisted victims of domestic violence in petition room filing for Orders of Protection. Provided advocacy, crisis intervention, and short-term counseling to victims of domestic violence. Provided clients with an orientation to Family Court and escorted clients to court as required. Assisted clients with direct services, such as shelters, relocation, transportation, public assistance, and referrals for long-term assistance.

Volunteer, Crisis Intervention Center, Glassboro, New Jersey, 1995-1997

REFERENCES

Dr. Sue Pervisor
Paterson Public Schools
Paterson, New Jersey 07509
(101) 555-0100

Mr. Abel Mentor
Eastside High School
Paterson, New Jersey 07509
(101) 555-0101

Dr. E. Val Waite
Glassboro State College
Glassboro, New Jersey 08028
(101) 555-0102

16

EXPERIENCED TEACHERS

MIKE KOPLOV

221 College Street Any City, State 12345 (101) 555-0008

TEACHING OBJECTIVE

TEACHER: Alternative high school setting stressing individualized instruction, goal-setting, counseling, and community-based partnerships.

CURRENT TEACHING EXPERIENCE

Alternative Center (Duval County Schools), Jacksonville, Florida, 1994 - present
Teach basic math, economics, computer science, and technology education to students in grades 7-12 in alternative setting. Teaching and advising responsibilities include:
- Create classroom environment conducive to learning and appropriate to maturity and interest of Center students
- Provide individualized instruction and counseling to Center students
- Supervise Center students throughout the campus and promote consistent and fair behavioral standards
- Design and revise math, economics, technology, and computer science curriculum
- Select with colleagues materials and resources appropriate for program's goals
- Assist in placement of students into traditional schools upon student's request
- Give regular technology training to all students using latest software/hardware
- Evaluate and select software in computer science and other curricular areas
- Provide training to staff for computer-assisted instruction and Internet applications
- Establish and maintain written and oral communication with parents

OTHER WORK

Paralegal Assistant, Fordham, Fordham, and Splunk, Miami, Florida, 1992 - 1994
Attached to individual corporate transactions to supervise and organize logistical matters throughout all aspects of transaction. Developed specialized databases for firm-wide and client use. Served as a resource to attorneys and clients in researching transactions.

ACTIVITIES AND MEMBERSHIPS

Executive Committee, local chapter of United Action for Youth
Teacher Representative, State Advisory Committee on Adult and Community Education
Member, Florida State Secondary Economics Council
Florida Teaching Profession-National Education Association
Membership Committee, Florida Association for Women in Computer Science

EDUCATION

M.A.   Exceptional Education - Florida State University, Tallahassee, Florida - 1997
B.S.   Economics - Bethune-Cookman College, Daytona Beach, Florida - 1992
A.S.   Computer Science - Miami-Dade Community College, Miami, Florida - 1990

References and Portfolio Available Upon Request

ROGER CHASE
221 College Street
Any City, State 12345
(101) 555-0009

TEACHING COMPETENCIES	Painting Printmaking Ceramics	Drawing Sculpture Art History

ACADEMIC TRAINING

Master of Arts in Teaching - Art Education, July 1999
Humboldt State University, Arcata, California

Bachelor of Science - Major in Art, Minor in African Studies, 1993
Memphis State University, Memphis, Tennessee

PROFESSIONAL TEACHING EXPERIENCE

Visual Arts Instructor, September 1999 - present
Performing Arts High School, Los Angeles, California
Magnet school operates year-round, with flexible hours. Students represent diverse ethnic and cultural backgrounds.
Teach painting, watercolor, ceramics to advanced students.
Team-teach course in humanities and the visual arts for advanced placement students in grades 11 and 12.
Developed optional after-school studio sessions and class review lessons in art history.
Supervise university students involved in semester-long internships and practicum assignments.

ADDITIONAL EXPERIENCE

Community Center for the Visual Arts, Adult Education Division, Los Angeles County, 2001 - present
Teach six-week courses in silversmithing, ceramics

CURRENT ACTIVITIES AND AFFILIATIONS

Member, Fine Arts Curriculum Development Committee, 1999-
Council Member, South Los Angeles Arts Council
Grant Recipient, Fine Arts Partnership Project
Treasurer, Black Action for Youth (BAY)
Member, National Art Teachers Association
Member, Los Angeles Academy of Fine Arts

CREDENTIALS

Career Development Center
Any City, State 12345
(101) 555-0008
FAX: (101) 555-0089

MARK WINDOM

221 College Street, Any City, State 12345
Home (101) 555-0009   School (101) 555-1111

OBJECTIVE
Teacher for At-Risk Students, Grades K-8

CURRENT PROFESSIONAL EXPERIENCE
Chapter I Teacher, Hattiesburg Public Schools, Hattiesburg, Mississippi, 1998 - present
Responsible for providing remediation in math and reading at MacKenzie Middle School.
Instructional strategies include extensive use of manipulatives and alternative assessment
techniques. Implement NCTM standards. Coordinate parent involvement programs.

FIELD EXPERIENCES
Elementary Math Student Teacher, Hattiesburg Public Schools, Fall semester 1996
Reading Clinic Practicum, Hattiesburg Catholic Schools, Spring semester 1996
Fourth-Grade Practicum, Hattiesburg Summer School Program, Summer 1995
> Responsibilities in these experiences included observing and assisting in all
> areas, working with individual students, organizing small group learning
> activities, tutoring remedial students, and evaluating student progress.

EDUCATION
Master of Arts in Education   University of Mississippi, 1998 - present
(in progress)   University, Mississippi

Bachelor of Science in Mathematics   University of Southern Mississippi, 1997
                                              Hattiesburg, Mississippi

GRADUATE COURSE CONCENTRATIONS
Learning Theories   Adolescent and Young Adult Learners
Behavioral Principles   Construction of Evaluation Instruments
Assessment of Young Children   Interventions and Referrals

PROFESSIONAL AFFILIATIONS
National Education Association   National Council of Teachers of Mathematics
Mississippi Council for Talented & Gifted   Regional Consortium for At-Risk Students

WORKSHOPS AND SEMINARS ATTENDED
At-Risk Students in Today's Classrooms: Symptoms and Solutions. Region 10 Consortium of
        Teachers and Social Workers, Atlanta, Georgia, March 1998
Students At-Risk: Reversing the Cycle of Educational Failure. State Education Convention,
        Mississippi Education Association, Jackson, Mississippi, February 1997
Conference sessions on topics of Whole Language, Reading Recovery, and Literacy
        International Reading Association Conference, San Antonio, Texas, March 1997

REFERENCES
Career Advising and Placement Center, Any City, State 12345   Telephone: (101) 555-0008

TARA SAGE

221 College Street
Any City, State 12345
(101) 555-0009 (home)
(101) 555-0005 (school)

PROFESSIONAL EXPERIENCE: 16 years
Eisenhower High School, Lawton, Oklahoma, 1991-2000
Business Education Teacher, grades 10-12
Yearbook advisor
Frederick High School, Frederick, Oklahoma, 1987-1991
Business Education Teacher, grades 9-12
Yearbook and student newspaper advisor
Temple Junior-Senior High School, Temple, Oklahoma, 1984-1987
Business Education and English Teacher, grades 9-12
Student newspaper advisor, assistant basketball coach

EXPERIENCE HIGHLIGHTS:
Teaching responsibilities include courses in:

Business Calculations	Business and Contract Law
Entrepreneurship	Record Keeping
Document Formatting	Document Production

Arranged for business internship opportunities and supervised student interns
Developed word processing short courses for faculty development series
Cooperating teacher for 11 student teachers and 8 practicum students

COMMITTEE RESPONSIBILITIES:
Faculty representative, Lawton School-Community Partnerships Study Group
Planning committee, Lawton High School Parent-Teacher Association
Computer Needs Assessment Task Force, Lawton High School
Writing Across the Curriculum Committee

PROFESSIONAL MEMBERSHIPS AND HONORS:
Nominated for Oklahoma Teacher of the Year, 1999
Outstanding Educator Award, Lawton Jaycees, 1997
Phi Delta Kappa, local chapter officer 1994-1998
Oklahoma Vocational Association
Oklahoma Educational Association

SELECTED PROFESSIONAL SEMINARS, 1992-PRESENT:
Desktop Publishing for Student Journalists
Methods of Alternative Assessment
Topics in Work Force Education
Technology for Restructuring Schools
Educational Technology for "At-Risk" Students

ACADEMIC BACKGROUND:
University of Oklahoma, Norman, Oklahoma
Graduate Studies - Curriculum and Instruction (Summers 1991, 1993)
Midwestern State University, Wichita Falls, Texas
B.A. in Business Education, 1984

REFERENCES AVAILABLE UPON REQUEST AT
Placement and Teacher Certification
Any City, State 12345
(101) 555-0008 FAX: (101) 555-1118

BERNARD JANSSEN
221 College Street
Any City, State 12345
(101) 555-0009

OBJECTIVE   Head Basketball Coach

EDUCATION   University of New Hampshire, Durham, New Hampshire
               M.A. Degree, Exercise Science, May 1999
                    Area of Specialization: Athletic Administration
               B.S. Degree, Physical Education and Mathematics, 1991

COACHING   Motivate and develop all-around student athletes, physically
STRENGTHS   and mentally
               Instill sportsmanship both on and off the court
               Thorough knowledge of basketball fundamentals
               Coordinate all program levels - elementary through varsity
               Initiate and maintain communications with parents, other
                    teachers, and school administrators
               Work with summer camp programs and promote athletes to
college recruiters

COACHING   Head Basketball Coach, Physical Education Teacher,
EXPERIENCE   Plymouth High School, Plymouth, Vermont, 1997-present
                    Records and accomplishments:
                    Class 3A division; 24 wins, 8 losses (1999)
                    State qualifiers; district champions (1998, 1999)
                    Three athletes named to All-Conference Academic Team
                    Players selected on 1st and 2nd All-Conference Teams
                    Named Conference Coach of the Year (1998)

               Shabazz High School, Newark, New Jersey, 1995-1997

               Hayward Military Academy, Rockford, Illinois, 1992-1995

               Record for these positions:
               Overall basketball record: 102 wins; 68 losses
               Honors include three Conference Champions, All-Conference
                    selections, and sportsmanship recognition
               Student athletes received college scholarship awards

CREDENTIALS Career Planning & Placement Service, Any City, State 12345
               (101) 555-0008   FAX: (101) 555-0089

KARLA LUDKE

221 College Street   Any City, State 12345   (101) 555-0009

TEACHING COMPETENCIES
- Computer Languages
  COBOL, FORTRAN, C++
- Keyboard/word processing
- Computer network administration
- In-service computer instruction
- Hardware/software evaluation
- Web page design
- Video editing/multimedia

EDUCATION

Bachelor of Science Degree, Major: Computer Science, 8/97
University of Wisconsin-Parkside, Kenosha, Wisconsin

Bachelor of Science Degree, Major: Mathematics, 1992-1996
Marshall University, Huntington, West Virginia
- Dean's List
- Vera Goode Scholarship, 1996

CLASSROOM TEACHING EXPERIENCE

H. S. Computer Science Teacher: Green Bay Public Schools, Green Bay, Wisconsin, 1998-present
Teach students at all levels of computer knowledge ranging from novice to the experienced high school programmer. Use a variety of teaching and motivational strategies to encourage students to reach their potential. Created a Computer Club, Senior Club (for advanced students), and a volunteer high school computer outreach team that visits senior citizens' centers to teach computer skills.

Computer Lab Supervisor: Lakeview Elementary, Kenosha, Wisconsin, 1996-1997
Supervised lab and instructed students from first grade through sixth grade. Designed special activities to demonstrate basic computer concepts and usage. Developed software to reinforce learning goals. Also developed and taught district-wide faculty computer mini-courses. Created a faculty computer resource center with ongoing instruction for grading programs, test development, and materials design. Responsible for the repair and maintenance of equipment.

RELATED EXPERIENCE

Computer Tutor, Kenosha and Green Bay, Wisconsin, 1996-present
Summer School Computer Instructor, Green Bay Summer Program, 1998-present
Committee Chair, Green Bay Public Schools Technology Committee, 1998-present
Faculty Representative, Region 8 Technology Evaluation Committee, 1998-present

PROFESSIONAL ORGANIZATIONS

International Association for Computer Information Systems
National Council of Teachers of Mathematics
National Education Association

Credentials available at the Career Center
Any City, State 12345   Telephone: (101) 555-0008

MOLLY WARD

221 College Street   Any City, State 12345   (101) 555-0009

TEACHING
EXPERIENCE:

Benton High School, St. Joseph, Missouri, 1997-present
Driver Education Teacher
Provide classroom instruction, simulation instruction, and behind-the-wheel laboratory practice on the road.

- Classroom instruction in basic and complex driving techniques and strategies, including personal and social responsibilities of drivers and inculcating safe driving habits
- Introduce driving simulator; supervise weekly simulator training for each student
- Schedule and carry out behind-the-wheel instruction to provide observation and actual driving practice for each student

Physical Education Teacher, 1993-1997

- Taught skills courses including team and individual sports and fitness activities
- Member of planning team to develop and implement coeducational Early Bird physical education classes for grades 11 and 12

COACHING
AND RELATED
ACTIVITIES:

Women's Golf-Assistant Coach, 1994-1996
Volleyball-Assistant Coach, 1993-1996
Senior Class Advisor, 1997-present

PROFESSIONAL
AFFILIATIONS:

Missouri Education Association
American Driver and Traffic Safety Education Association
American Alliance for Health, Physical Education,
    Recreation, and Dance
Pi Lambda Theta

SPECIAL
INTERESTS:

Tennis
Classic and antique automobile restoration and repair

EDUCATIONAL
BACKGROUND:

Driver Education-Certification Program, 1997
Northwest Missouri State University, Maryville, Missouri

Physical Education-Bachelor's Degree, 1992
College of the Ozarks, Point Lookout, Missouri

CREDENTIALS
AVAILABLE:

Education Division
Any City, State 12345
Telephone: (101) 555-0008

CARLO SANDOR

221 College Street Any City, State 12345
Home: (101) 555-0009   School: (101) 545-0005

PROFESSIONAL TEACHING EXPERIENCE

- Grades 1-3, departmentalized, cross-graded, team-teaching
    Hanover County Public Schools, Ashland, Virginia, 1993-1999
- Classroom Teacher, grade 2, multidisciplinary team member
    Goose Creek Independent Schools, Baytown, Texas, 1990-1993

CURRENT PROFESSIONAL SERVICE

Organized whole language district in-service activities for K-6 teachers
Designed science curriculum; developed science centers for primary units
Chaired planning committee for Multicultural Non-Sexist curriculum
Supervised reading clinicians from the Virginia Reading Clinic
Trained and mentored university student teachers and practicum students
Conducted parent education classes for the district Parent Seminar Series

COMMITTEE LEADERSHIP

District Reading Committee, Hanover County
Hanover County ELP (Extended Learning Program) Committee
PTA Faculty Representative-Goose Creek and Hanover County
Task Force Co-leader-School/Community Collaboration Efforts

PROFESSIONAL MEMBERSHIPS AND HONORS

Jaycee's Outstanding Young Educator   KCNA-TV Apple Award
International Reading Association   National Education Association
Council on Effective Teaching   Virginia Association of Teachers

ACADEMIC BACKGROUND

Graduate Studies-Curriculum and Instruction, 1997-present
    Mary Washington College, Fredricksburg, Virginia
B.S.-Elementary Education, 1993, Southwest Texas State University
    San Marcos, Texas
A.A. Liberal Arts, 1990, Austin Community College, Austin, Texas

References Available Upon Request

TERI J. KING
221 College Street
Any City, State 12345
(101) 555-0009

SPECIAL STRENGTHS
- Collaborative team-teaching approach   • Multiage groupings   • Integrated curriculum

PROFESSIONAL CLASSROOM EXPERIENCE

Iowa City Community School District, Iowa City, Iowa

Longfellow Elementary-Grades 5 and 6, August 1989 to present

Team member responsible for leadership in mathematics for four-person unit teaching multiage classes including SCI and ESL students. Special responsibilities include:
- demonstration classroom for use of integrated curriculum using cooperative learning, hands-on use of manipulatives, and constructivist strategies
- schedule planning to maximize blocked instructional and common planning time
- organize and implement special events in areas of mathematics, language arts, social studies, drama, creative expression, and environmental education

Northwest Junior High-Math Maintenance, Summer 1996

Team-taught math concepts on an individual basis

EDUCATION

The University of Iowa, Iowa City, Iowa

Ph.D. Program in Elementary Education, 1997-

University of Northern Iowa, Cedar Falls, Iowa

M.A. 1993, Elementary and Middle School Mathematics

B.A. 1988, Elementary and Middle School Education

INTERNATIONAL EDUCATION EXPERIENCES

University of London, London, England

American Institute of Foreign Study Semester Abroad. Fall 1986

Oxford University, Oxford, England

International Student Leadership Program, Summer 1987

LEADERSHIP AND SERVICE

Longfellow Elementary School: Student Council Advisor, Safety Patrol Supervisor, Math Olympiad, Grade Level Unit Leader, Technology Committee, Scheduling Committee, Staffing Ratio Committee, Child Study Team, School Improvement Team, Phase III Committee, Building Handbook Committee, Conflict Resolution Training

Iowa City Community School District: Facilitator for Middle Grades Study Group on Transitions, Middle Grades Committee Curriculum Review for Media/Literature, Co-author of Mathematics Scope and Sequence, Curriculum writer for Voyage of the Mimi I Literature Unit and Phyllis Reynolds Naylor author study

Professional: Presenter at National Council of Teachers of Mathematics Conference and Iowa Council of Teachers of Mathematics Conference in Des Moines, Iowa, Presenter at University of Northern Iowa Mathematics Conference, Facilitator for Young Writer's Conference at Cornell College

SELECTED PROFESSIONAL DEVELOPMENT

Site-based Shared Decision Making

Training includes background of effective school research, development of decision-making skills and overview of school improvement process.

Conflict Management

Training included planning for student and staff training, methods of record keeping, and program evaluation.

Study Group Facilitators

Training included the roles and responsibilities of study group facilitators, as well as review of research on the effectiveness of study groups in the field of education.

Nonviolent Crisis Intervention

Training included nonviolent interventions for crisis situations in the classroom.

RELATED TEACHING EXPERIENCE

The University of Iowa, Iowa City, Iowa

Belin/Blank International Center for Gifted Education - CHESS Instructor

Math problem solving, Summers 1994-1996

Private Tutor, Fall 1989-present

Provide one-on-one instruction in the area of math and reading for grades 2-11

Graduate Assistant, UNI Mathematics Education Department, Spring 1989

Assisted with instruction of elementary mathematics methods courses for pre-education majors, provided tutorial assistance in math help sessions, assisted professors with research projects

Preschool Assistant, Chelsea Open Aire Nursery School, Chelsea, England. Fall 1986

— PENC -Prof. Edu. of N. Carin

AWARDS AND AFFILIATIONS

Kate Wickham Scholarship Honoree

National Council of Teachers of Mathematics

Iowa Council of Teachers of Mathematics

Iowa Reading Association

Iowa City Education Association

Phi Delta Kappa

Kappa Mu Epsilon

Kappa Delta Pi

References Available Upon Request

NINA LERNER

221 College Street
Any City, State 12345
(101) 555-0009

OBJECTIVE

Elementary Departmentalized Math
Skills in creative problem-solving, technology applications, and specialized math software

EDUCATIONAL BACKGROUND

University of Arkansas-Little Rock   1995-1998   B.S. Elementary Education
Little Rock, Arkansas   *Areas of Specialization:*
       Mathematics and Science

MATHEMATICS AND SCIENCE-COURSES OF INTEREST

Calculus I & II	Organic Chemistry I & II	Physics
Linear Algebra	Anatomy and Physiology	Microbiology
Computing with FORTRAN	Statistics	

TEACHING EXPERIENCE

Stowe Elementary School, Fort Worth School District, Fort Worth, Texas, August 1993-present
Classroom Teacher-Grade 2 and Departmentalized Math
Taught in both a self-contained and departmentalized classroom setting; utilized the methods of The Writing Process, whole language, and the integrated language arts; applied a variety of math problem-solving techniques; field-tested new math curriculum. Activities included: First-Grade Math Bee Coordinator, Social Committee Chairperson, Campus Coordinating Committee Member, Fort Worth Teachers' and Community Advocacy Committee Representative.

Amon Carter Jr. YMCA, Fort Worth, Texas, Summer 1993
Coordinator and Instructor-"Live and Learn," a program for middle school students identified as at-risk. Designed and presented life-skill lessons through group discussions, guest speakers, field trips, and active participation. Actively involved business leaders in life-skill program.

Eisenhower Elementary School, Little Rock School District, Little Rock, Arkansas, Spring 1991
Student Teacher-Grade 4
Developed and taught poetry unit; instructed and supervised computer lab; worked with individuals in math; introduced and helped maintain daily journal writing; helped organize an all-school environmental awareness project.

Hoover Elementary School, Fayetteville School District, Fayetteville, Arkansas, Fall 1989
Practicum Teacher-Grade 6
Experience focused primarily on science instruction. Developed and taught science lessons; assisted with computer activities and individual work in math and science.

PROFESSIONAL DEVELOPMENT COURSES

Classroom Management	Peer Coaching	Improving Student Writing
Quest	NASA Math	Newspapers in Education

CREDENTIALS at Teacher Career Center
Any City, State 12345 Telephone: (101) 555-0008

MO ABU-SHAKRA

221 College Street
Any City, State 12345
(101) 555-0009

STRENGTHS

Creative Writing	Adolescent Literature	African-American Literature
Portfolio Assessment	Technology Integration	Journalistic Writing

EDUCATION

M.A. Degree   Writer's Workshop, The Pennsylvania State University, Summers 1999-present
B.A. Degree   Major: English   Minors: Spanish, Journalism, Temple University, August 1998
A.A. Degree   Major: Computer Programming, Valley Community College, Pittsburgh, May 1996

TEACHING EXPERIENCES

High School English and Journalism, University High School, University Park, PA, August 1998-present
- Teach in a collaborative setting with 18 professionals. Plan cross-curricular units with science, math, and social studies departments. Use technology extensively to introduce new materials to students, to supplement traditional library research, and to teach basic layout design for newspaper and yearbook. Create and instruct units on early American authors including minority authors. Conference with students regarding writing and journal projects and final portfolio submissions.

Middle School Language Arts and Drama, Student Teaching, Concord Middle School, Cranston, RI, Fall 1998
- Worked in a team-teaching unit with sixth- and seventh-grade students using block scheduling (90-minute periods on A,B schedules.) Units on grammar, basic writing, and contemporary literature were developed by the team and supplemented with technology infusion, guest speakers, and cooperative learning.

RELATED YOUTH EMPLOYMENT

Youth Crisis Counselor, Campus Crisis Services, Temple University, 1997-1998
>   Answer emergency calls, counsel and advise clients, and make appropriate referrals to college and community-based agencies. Work with all ages from the teen-line to the adult-line.

Camp Counselor, Camp Courageous, Mount St. Clair, Pennsylvania, summers 1996-1997
>   Worked with students with severe physical disabilities ranging in age from 5 to 25 years.
>   Activities included horseback riding, boating and water activities, and crafts. Lived in
>   cabin with campers and provided a comfortable, encouraging, and safe environment.

SERVICE

Committee member, Technology Integration Team, University High School, 1999-present
Co-Chair and Student Liaison to Vice President, Campus RiverFest, Penn State University, 1999
Elected Senator, Student Government, Renow Residence Hall, Temple University, 1996-1997

References and portfolio materials available upon request.

Clayton Crizmann

221 College Street, Any City, State 12345 (101) 555-0009
ccriz@kc.sch.us

COMPETENCIES:
- Teach German to students at all levels in traditional and transitional settings
- Design German curriculum for elementary, middle school, and secondary programs
- Develop bilingual learning centers focusing on middle school students
- Contributing member to teams and collaborative teaching approaches
- Create bilingual publications for school and community

PROFESSIONAL TEACHING EXPERIENCE:
German, grades 1-4 (1996-1999); grades 9-12 (current responsibility)
     Kansas City Public Schools, Kansas City, Missouri, 1997-present
German, Middle School Grades 5-7
     San Antonio Independent Schools, San Antonio, Texas, 1995-1997
Bilingual, Transitional Elementary Grades 4-6
     Saint Louis Independent Schools, St. Louis, Missouri, 1993-1995

COMMITTEE LEADERSHIP:

Co-chair, German Curriculum Revision Project	Kansas City Bilingual Consortium
Representative—Superintendent's Council	District Committee for Magnet Schools

PROFESSIONAL MEMBERSHIPS:

Missouri Association of Teachers of German	American Association of Teachers of German
International German Student Society	American Federation of Teachers

RECENT PROFESSIONAL DEVELOPMENT SEMINARS (since 1996):
Language Learning Centers for Elementary Students, University of Chicago
Midwest Regional Students-At-Risk Symposium, Washington University
Missouri Native Language Project, University of Missouri-Columbia

ACADEMIC BACKGROUND:
University of Missouri-Kansas City, Kansas City, Missouri
     Graduate studies in ESL and Bilingual Education, 1998-present
Black Hills State University, Spearfish, South Dakota
     B.A., German and Elementary Education, 1993

REFERENCES:
Available from Placement and Teacher Certification, Any City, State 12345 (101) 555-0008

DORIS ANNE WILKEN
221 College Street Any City, State 12345
(101) 555-0008

TEACHING STRENGTHS

- Recognize and encourage students who are talented to explore and discover
- Work with teachers and parents to deal more effectively with gifted children
- Teach colleagues how to adapt learning materials for classroom use
- Help students develop a heightened sense of social responsibility for their talents

---

EDUCATION

M.A.-Gifted Education-Eastern Kentucky University, Richmond, Kentucky-1998
Certification Program-Elementary Education-Ohio University, Athens, Ohio-1993
B.A.-Music Performance, Voice-Valparaiso University, Valparaiso, Indiana-1992

TEACHING EXPERIENCE

Teacher, Extended Learning Program-Marion City Schools, Marion, Ohio, 1997 -
- Work directly with elementary students as an enrichment facilitator.
- Conduct student assessment, and provide in-service for educators and parents.
- Work with ELP Teacher Committees to schedule and coordinate school visits by speakers, visiting artists, and field experiences for large and small groups.
- Facilitate enrichment experiences for students interested in more in-depth exploration of a topic.
- Develop and conduct enrichment lessons and units, with particular emphasis on music and performing arts.
- Participate in Extended Learning Program Advisory Committee.

Teacher-Grades 4-6, Indian Mound Elementary School, Marion, Ohio, 1993-1996
- Taught reading, language arts, mathematics, and science in grade 4; music in grades 4-6 in semi-departmentalized setting.

RECENT PROFESSIONAL DEVELOPMENT

National Conference:
Henry B. & Jocelyn Wallace National Research Symposium on Talent Development, Connie Belin National Center for Gifted Education, The University of Iowa, Iowa City, Iowa, 1999

Presentations:
"Identification of Gifted Minority Students," Conference on Gifted, Southern Illinois University, Carbondale, 1998
"Gender Roles: Impact on Giftedness," Great Lakes Seminar, Ohio University, Athens, 1997

References and portfolio materials available upon request

CRAIG OVERLAND

221 College Street
Any City, State 12345
(101) 555-0009

Teaching Interests

MATHEMATICS

Pre-Algebra, Algebra, Advanced Algebra
Geometry, Trigonometry & Finite Mathematics
Pre-Calculus, Calculus

Professional Teaching Experience

Mathematics, Newnan High School, Newnan, Georgia, 9/95-present
Teach one section of Advanced Placement Mathematics, two sections of Geometry, and two sections of Advanced Algebra; encourage students to use scientific calculators and assist with their use; incorporate significant amounts of Algebra in Geometry courses, and introduced proofs in a flow-chart format.

College Algebra Instructor, Newnan Center of West Georgia College, 1999
As adjunct faculty member, taught two semesters of Beginning Algebra and two semesters of Intermediate Algebra to adult college students enrolled in evening classes through the Division of Continuing Education of West Georgia College.

Beginning Algebra course encompassed material similar to a first-year high school Algebra course including real numbers, linear equations, factoring, exponents, and simple graphing.
Intermediate Algebra covered material comparable to a second-year high school Algebra course, including functions and graphing, polynomials, solving inequalities, second degree equations, systems of equations, and logarithms.

Current Activities and Affiliations

Co-chair, Newnan High School Curriculum Review Committee
Board member, Georgia Council of Teachers of Mathematics (GCTM)
Member, National Council of Teachers of Mathematics
Awarded GCTM Grant for Advanced Placement Teacher Training
Founding Member, Metropolitan Area Mathematics Club

Academic Training

University of Georgia Athens, Georgia	M.A., 1995	Mathematics Education
Augusta College Augusta, Georgia	B.S., 1988	Major: Mathematics Minor: Computer Science

Credentials

Office of Career Planning
Any City, State 12345 (101) 555-0008

SONJA WELLES
221 College Street, Any City, State 12345
(101) 555-0009 (home)   (101) 545-0005 (school)

PROFESSIONAL TEACHING EXPERIENCE: 10 years

Mayville-Portland School District, Mayville, North Dakota, 1995-present
Instrumental Music Teacher and Department Chair, Mayville High School

Devils Lake School District 1, Devils Lake, North Dakota, 1993-1994
Instrumental and Vocal Teacher, Central Junior Senior High School

Mustang Independent School District, Mustang, Oklahoma, 1990-1993
Instrumental Music Teacher, Mustang High School

EXPERIENCE HIGHLIGHTS:

Organized and hosted the first statewide junior high honor band festival
Developed creative contemporary marching band scores for three marching bands
Received highest honors at the North Dakota State Marching Band Contest
Evaluated curriculum for three districts and revived programs with new ideas
Chosen as the top high school jazz band in North Dakota, 1998

CURRENT LEADERSHIP:

President, State Bandmasters Association
Faculty Liaison, Fine Arts Committee for Music Improvement in North Dakota
State Delegate, National Education Association Convention, Los Angeles

PROFESSIONAL MEMBERSHIPS:

Percussive Arts Society   American Bandmasters Association
National Education Association   American School Band Directors' Association

ACADEMIC BACKGROUND:

Mayville State University, Mayville, North Dakota
M.A. Performance and Conducting, 1997
University of North Dakota, Grand Forks, North Dakota
B.M. Instrumental Music Education, Specialty: Percussion, 1989

HONORS AND ACTIVITIES:

Selected Outstanding Music Teacher of the Year, North Dakota, 1998
Awarded Outstanding Graduate Student in Music Education, 1996
Member, North Dakota Symphony Orchestra
Percussion Ensemble, Symphony Orchestra, Marching Band

REFERENCES AVAILABLE UPON REQUEST AT
Career Planning & Placement Center, Any City, State 12345
Phone: (101) 555-0008   FAX: (101) 555-1118

NINA CHAVEZ-HOUSTON

221 College Street   Any City, State 12345   (101) 555-0008

COMPETENCIES

- Bilingual-Spanish
- Knowledgeable about migrant family educational needs
- Establish and maintain strong working relationships with social service agencies
- Collaborate with staff members in designing appropriate individual educational plans
- Train and supervise aides and volunteer helpers

PROFESSIONAL EXPERIENCE

Parent Involvement Teacher
Trinidad School District, Trinidad, Colorado, 1992-
Promote effective involvement of parents of preschool children in program services and
   child development
Serve as liaison with Migrant Child and Family Service
Make referrals to agencies addressing health, nutrition, social service, or other needs
   of migrant children
Plan and conduct parenting classes in English and Spanish for parents of migrant children

RELATED EXPERIENCE

Child Welfare Case Aide
Kit Carson County Social Services, Burlington, Colorado, 1990-1992
Assisted caseworkers in providing assistance to children of migrant families; handled routine
client inquiries and made referrals to caseworker or other local or state agencies; translated
Spanish/English as required.

EDUCATION

B.S.-Elementary Education, College of Santa Fe, Santa Fe, New Mexico, 1987-1990
   Emphasis: Early Childhood Education
   Minor: Sociology

A.A.-Child Development, Aims Community College, Greeley, Colorado, 1985-1987
   Dean's List

REFERENCES

Available upon request.

T.J. TRACH

221 College Street
Any City, State 12345 (101) 555-0009

TEACHING AND COACHING COMPETENCIES

CLASSROOM
Physical Education
Health Education
General Science

COACHING
Wrestling
Track
Summer Baseball

EXTRACURRICULAR INTERESTS

Booster Club Coordinator
Fund-raising Organizer

Weight Lifting Club Sponsor
Intramural Sponsor

CLASSROOM TEACHING

H.S. Physical Education and Health, East Bay High School, Seattle, January 1998-
Responsibilities include teaching units in the following areas:
• Health Awareness Issues • Physical Education, all grade levels • Coed Weight Lifting
• Physical Fitness & Weight Control • Seminar on AIDS • Nutrition • Exercise as Leisure
Responsibilites include working as part of a collaborative team member using a 90-minute
Block Schedule. Use a variety of teaching stratetgies to motivate and challenge a diverse student
population. Active participant in department and building committees.

PRACTICUM EXPERIENCE

Geriatric Leisure Activities, Bellevue Community Center, Bellevue, Spring 1997
• Assisted with all leisure activities involving senior citizens from a two-county area
• Organized and led small group activities in exercising, swimming, and aerobics
• Involved in daily contact with volunteers, administrators, and senior citizens

ACTIVITIES AND AFFILIATIONS

Baseball Coach, East Bay High School, 1998-present; Wrestling Coach, 1999
All-Conference Selection, Wrestling, Gonzaga University, 1997 and 1998
Baseball Coach and Umpire, Spokane Summer Recreation League, 1997-1998
Fund-raiser & Benefit Chair, Washington Heart Association, 1997-present

ACADEMIC TRAINING

Gonzaga University, Spokane, Washington, Bachelor of Science Degree, May 1997
Major: Leisure Studies   Minor: Health Education
Credentials available at Center for Career Services, Any City, State 12345 (101) 555-0008

MARY CLAUSSEN

221 College Street, Any City, State 12345 (101) 555-0009

COMPETENCIES

Science: Chemistry, Biology, Earth Science, Environmental Studies
Technology: Windows Environment; Web Design and Basic Programming
Magnet School: Experience working in a specialized setting

**PROFESSIONAL
EXPERIENCE**

Teacher, Technology & Science High School, Wichita, 1996-present
Teach upper-level science courses in chemistry, biology, and environmental studies.
Magnet school has a multicultural student body operating as an all-year-round
school with flexible hours. Teach vocational science courses preparing students for
the world of work and teach advanced studies to college-bound students. Supervise
students participating in internships with local businesses and hold regular seminars
with corporate sponsors.

Freelance Consultant, Web Design Specalist, 1995-present
Web sites construction for business and educational clients, including the design and
customization of CGI applications. Provide training for clients to edit and design
business Web sites. See Web site at: www.design.com

**INTERNSHIP
EXPERIENCE**

Middle School Science, Westfield Middle School, Wichita, Spring 1996
High School Chemistry, Cambridge Academy, Kansas City, 1995
Outward Bound-Oregon, Wilderness Program, Greenwich, 1993

**ACADEMIC
TRAINING**

Wichita State University, Master of Arts in Teaching, 1996, Science Education
Boston University, Bachelor of Science Degree, 1993, Majors: Biology, Math

**CURRENT
ACTIVITIES**

Chair, Technology Department, 1998-present
Council Member, Superintendent's Roundtable, 1998-present
Grant recipient, Environmental Studies Collaboration Project
   (project includes five districts and Wichita State, 1997-present)
Member, Collegiate Curriculum Review Committee, 1997
President, State Sierra Club, 1997

AFFILIATIONS

Member, National Science Teachers Association
Member, Academy of Science

CREDENTIALS

Credentials available at Office of Career Planning Any City, State 12345

ALEXANDER ANTONIO

Present Address: School Address:
221 College Street   30 Royal Avenue
Any City 12345   Mytown, State 23456
(101) 555-0009   (909) 333-0003

TEACHING OBJECTIVE AND SKILLS
Social Studies Instructor; Cocurricular Sponsor; Athletic Coach
• Challenge and motivate students in a multicultural setting
• Utilize effective classroom management and discipline strategies
• Create and implement interdisciplinary materials
• Implement innovative instructional plans (community resources,
  case studies, simulations, field trips, computer instruction)
• Participate actively in team instructional and cocurricular planning

ACADEMIC BACKGROUND
University of Missouri-Columbia, Columbia, Missouri
    Graduate Studies, College of Education, 1998-present
    Bachelor of Arts Degree, 1992 Major: Social Studies Education
    Dean's List, Daren Goode Undergraduate Geography Scholarship

CLASSROOM TEACHING EXPERIENCE
Hickman Senior High School, Columbia, Missouri   1997-present
Pruitt Military Academy, St. Louis, Missouri   1992-1997
Summer Learning Program, St. Louis, Missouri   Summer 1996

Responsibilities during the above teaching positions included:
• Taught courses including Geography, Latin America, World Cultures, American History
• Participated in daily team meetings to plan and implement interdisciplinary teaching units
• Worked with English, Science, and Art in designing curricula for Latin American
  interdisciplinary materials
• Developed prototype for district-wide portfolio for student academic assessment
• Encouraged parents to volunteer and participate in their student's learning and in activities
• Helped parents organize volunteer action groups and work with administrative teams

COACHING EXPERIENCE
Cross-country Head Coach, Hickman High School, 1998-present
Track & Cross-country Head Coach, Pruitt Academy, 1995-1997
Boys Club Track Volunteer Coach, St. Louis, 1992-1995
City Track Club Sprint Coach, St. Louis, 1990-1995
    (Three Conference Championships, Cross-country State Title,
    numerous all-conference selections, Conference Coach of-the-Year
    Award-1998, three sprinters invited to Olympic trials)

A. Antonio
page 2

COCURRICULAR EXPERIENCES
Academic Decathlon Sponsor, 4 years   National Geography Bee Coach, 2 years
Student Senate Advisor, 4 years   International Club Sponsor, 2 years
History Fair Sponsor, 3 years   Junior Historian Club Advisor, 1 year

COMMITTEE AND WORKSHOP ACTIVITIES
• Interdisciplinary Committee Chair, Hickman High School
• Social Studies Curriculum Review Committee Member, Columbia Schools
• Site-based Decision Making Committee Member, Hickman High School
• Workshop Leader, New Staff In-service-training, St. Louis
• NCA Evaluation Team Member, Blue Springs High Schools

MEMBERSHIPS AND LICENSURE
National Council for Social Studies   American Federation of Teachers
State Social Studies Council   Missouri Historian's Council
Teaching Licenses-Missouri & Kansas   Coaching Endorsements-Missouri, Kansas, Iowa

COMMUNITY ACTIVITIES
Fund-raiser, Greater Columbia Area for Disabled   Board Member, Columbia United Way
Media Marathon Volunteer   American Heart Association
Troop Leader, Brownie Scout Troop #121   Crop Walk Volunteer

ATHLETIC RECOGNITION
• All-American-Track   • First Team All-Conference   • Team Captain
• Most Valuable Player   • MVP, Drake Relays   • Academic All-Big Eight

PLACEMENT FILE
Credentials: Career Planning & Placement, Any City, State 12345 (101) 555-0008

JULIET STRAUSS
221 College Street
Any City, State 12345
(101) 555-1111

DEGREES

M.A. Special Education, Texas Woman's University, Denton, Texas June 1997
  Thesis: Community Mobility of Emotionally Disturbed Teenagers in Group Home Settings
  Advisor: Dr. Will B. Prof, Department Chair
B.A. Special Education Emphasis: Behavior Disorders May 1989

CLASSROOM EXPERIENCE

Special Education Teacher, grades 10-12, Special Services Alternative Center, Dallas, Texas, August 1997–present. Case manager for emotionally and behaviorally disturbed students removed from local high school programs. Responsibilities include interfacing with outside referral agencies on behalf of students, coordinating the instructional programs, developing appropriate Individual Education Plans, and designing and monitoring specialized behavior management programs.

Special Education Teacher, grades 7 and 8, Connally Independent School District, Waco, Texas, 1995–1996. Self-contained with integration classroom for emotionally disturbed students. Major teaching responsibilities included reading, mathematics, and social studies. Implemented initial stages of the special education immersion program placing students in regular academic classrooms.

Special Education Teacher, grades 5-12, North Texas Residential Care Center, Dallas, Texas, 1991–1995. Semi-residential placement center for emotionally disturbed students ages 10 to 18. Teaching responsibilities included all curricular areas. Assisted psychologist in assessment of students with behavioral or emotional problems.

UNIVERSITY ASSISTANTSHIP

Supervisor of Student Teachers, Texas Woman's University, Denton, Texas, 1996–1997.
Supervised undergraduate special education student teachers in three school districts. Provided guidance to students regarding their instructional techniques and overall classroom performances during semester-long internship experience.

RELATED WORK EXPERIENCE

Systems Unlimited Inc., Dallas, Texas, 1989–1991
  Teacher for Summer Program, 1989–1991
  Planned activities for 12-16-year-old behavior disorder students.
  Family and Child Trainer, 1989–1991
  Provided 24-hour care for three severe/profound girls ages four to six.
  Direct Care Staff, 1989–1990
  Charged with the complete care of five severe/profound disabled teenagers
  in a group home setting.

PRESENTATIONS

"Evaluation of Video Feedback as a Training Procedure for BD Students." Poster presentation
  at the Convention for the Association for Behavior Analysis, Phoenix, Arizona, April 1999.
"Alternative Settings for Success." Presentation at the Texas Special Education Conference, San
  Antonio, Texas, November 1998.
"Community Mobility and Special Populations." Breakout session facilitator, Special Education
  Regional Convention, Corpus Christi, Texas, May 1997.

References provided upon request.

17

SPECIAL SERVICES

JORDAN WUKO
221 College Street • Any City, State 12345 • (101)555-0009 •j-wuko@oregonst.edu

ACADEMIC BACKGROUND
Oregon State University-Corvallis, B.S. Degree, Major: Athletic Training, Minor: Biology, 1999
Member, National Athletic Trainers Association, Oregon Athletic Trainers Society
Evergreen State College, Summer 1999, Student Trainer Clinic, Olympia, Washington

COURSES OF INTEREST
Medical Supervision of Athletics	Biomechanics of Human Motion
Counseling for Related Professions	Contemporary Nutrition
Diagnostic Techniques and Treatment	Clinical Sciences in Athletic Training

STUDENT TRAINING EXPERIENCES
Athletic Trainer Internship, Capital High School, Olympia, Washington, Fall 1999
Responsibilities included triage coverage of football team consisting of 70 athletes in grades 10 through 12. Experience gained in injury rehabilitation programs, first-aid applications, fluid replacement, practice supervision, and facility maintenance.

Student Trainer, Oregon State University, Corvallis, Oregon, 1998-1999
Responsibilities as a student trainer for various men's and women's sports; involved in all aspects of the college's training program including diagnosis, treatment, and rehabilitation.

TEAM EXPERIENCE
Volleyball: Training Camp, 1999; Conference Tournament and Conference Finals, 1998
Tennis: Team Coverage and Oregon Invitational Meet, 1998
Football: Team Coverage, 1998; Spring Scrimmage, 1997
Soccer: Home Games and Regional Finals, 1997

REHABILITATION EXPERIENCE
Rehabilitation program involved treatment strategies, evaluation consultations, and follow-up treatment for various sports. Observed three major surgical procedures for knee, shoulder, and ankle injuries. Special personal skills include swimmers' shoulder problems, ACL knee reconstruction, joint mobilization, and post-operative rehabilitation.

RELATED SUMMER WORK EXPERIENCES
Tennis	Oregon State University Summer Camps	1998
Basketball	Oregon High School Basketball Camps	1997-1998
Coach	Corvallis City Softball League	1996-1997

DISTINCTIONS
Oregon State University's Dean's List, 1999	Outstanding Student Trainer Award, 1999
Olympia Club Scholarship, 1997	All-State High School Swimmer, 2 years

References available upon request

EMILIA BURKE

221 College Street   Any City, State 12345   (101) 555-0009

STRENGTHS
- Assessment of students using appropriate diagnostic measures
- Experience with a wide range of exceptional educational needs
- Consult with classroom teachers, staff, and parents regarding special services, treatment plans, and referrals
- Experience with adaptive technologies

ACADEMIC BACKGROUND
M.S. Audiology, June 1999 Colorado State University-Fort Collins
B.S. Speech & Hearing, May 1997 University of Colorado-Boulder

COURSE HIGHLIGHTS

Pediatric Audiology	Tests and Measurements
Remedial Methods	Clinical Audiology
Rehabilitative Audiology	Hearing Aids I, II

PRACTICUM EXPERIENCES
Northeast Board of Cooperative Educational Services, Longmont, Colorado, January-May 1999
Participated in identification program for hearing disorders, including kindergarten screening. Select and implement therapy strategies for modifying communicative behavior of students with hearing problems. Participated in conferences with teachers and parents to foster communication and to develop appropriate intervention strategies.

Colorado School for the Deaf and the Blind, Colorado Springs, Fall 1998
Observe and assist with evaluation of children for hearing impairment, confer with physicians, parents, and technicians regarding hearing aids or other appropriate treatment and therapy.

RELATED EMPLOYMENT
Colorado Lions Camp, Woodland Park, Colorado-Summers 1996-1997
Residential counselor for hearing-impaired campers, ages 8-16; assist with recreational activities including backpacking, hiking, overnight camping.

MEMBERSHIPS
American Speech and Hearing Association
Colorado Audiology Students' Association

REFERENCES
Available upon request.

IVY JONES
221 College Street
Any City, State 12345
(101) 555-0009

OBJECTIVE

Counselor: Elementary (K-6) or Secondary (7-12)

EDUCATION

University of Nevada-Reno
  M.A. Degree-May 1999
    Counseling and Human Development
    Area of Specialization: School Counseling
  B.A. Degree-August 1993
    Home Economics Education and Spanish

COUNSELING SKILLS

Provide individual counseling
Facilitate small group counseling sessions
Conduct classroom guidance activities
Consult with parents, teachers, and community specialists
Coordinate outreach services to families
Use bilingual counseling skills (Spanish)

COUNSELING EXPERIENCE

Middle School Counselor, 4th-7th grades, Lake Tahoe School, 9/99-present

Responsibilities:
• Create a positive and supportive school counseling climate
• Initiate conflict management action groups for students
• Organize before-school sessions for new students
• Implement student-centered lunch seminars on topics dealing
  with coping skills, grief and loss, study habits, and AIDS
• Incorporate peer counseling skills into 6th-grade curriculum
• Use a variety of intervention techniques for at-risk students
• Provide resource materials for students exploring careers
• Initiate and conduct parent-teacher-counselor conferences at student's home

7th-12th grades Counseling Internship, Mountain High School, 2/98-4/98

Responsibilities:
• Administered and scored individualized achievement tests and
  assisted students in preparation for college admissions examinations
• Met with students on a regular basis to discuss career options
• Designed and maintained progress charts for students on suspension
• Conducted a student needs analysis survey of all high school grades
• Attended Student Study Team meetings and staffings for students
  on school suspension or parole

RELATED ACTIVITIES

Advisor to Board of Directors, Domestic Violence Abuse Shelter, 1998-present
Volunteer, Hispanic Community Center, 1998-present
Member, American Counseling Association
President, Reno Youth Shelter Foundation, 1996

CREDENTIALS

Career Development and Advising Office
Any City, State 12345 (101) 555-0008 FAX: (101) 555-0089

ALEXIS KARAMAN

221 College Street   Any City, State 12345
(101) 555-0009

COUNSELING COMPETENCIES

Crisis Intervention   Group & Individual Therapy   Multicultural Counseling
Chemical/ Substance Abuse   Conflict Management   Self-esteem & Relationship Skills

COUNSELING EXPERIENCE

Crisis Counselor and Substance Abuse Specialist
    King High School and Alternative Center, Detroit Public Schools, 1998-present
Middle School Counselor
    Riverside Intermediate School, Dearborn Heights Public Schools, 1995-1997
Crisis Intervention Counselor and Youth Advocate
    Youth Emergency Shelter, Detroit, Michigan, Summers 1995-present

Responsibilities in the above positions included:
• Implementation of crisis intervention counseling programs and activities at all levels
• Collaboration with mental health agencies and community resources to provide services
  for students and families
• Coordination with state and local programs in chemical abuse projects
• Development of various programs to assist students with personal and family crises

CLASSROOM EXPERIENCE

Journalism Teacher, junior/senior division, Affirmative Action Liaison; Yearbook Video Advisor
    Ford High School, Detroit Public Schools, 1992-1995
Journalism, Drama and Debate Teacher, Community Action Club Advisor; Peer Tutoring Coordinator
    East Catholic High School, Detroit, Michigan, 1990-1992

PROFESSIONAL AFFILIATIONS

National Counselor Certification Board
Association for Multicultural Counseling and Development
American Association for Counseling and Development
Michigan Association for Counseling and Development
National Education Association and Michigan State Education Association

EDUCATIONAL BACKGROUND

Wayne State University, Detroit, Michigan
    Bachelor of Arts Degree, 1990 Major: Journalism; Minor: African Studies
    Master of Arts Degree, 1995 School Counseling; Emphases: Counseling & Substance Abuse

CREDENTIALS

Education Placement Office, Any City, State 12345   (101) 555-0008 FAX: (101) 555-0089

Alexis Karaman
page 2

PROFESSIONAL ACCOMPLISHMENTS

PROFESSIONAL SERVICE, 1996-Present

Conferences Attended:
Regional Crisis Intervention Consortium, Chicago, July 1999
Associative Disorder-Multiple Personalities Conference, St. Louis, May 1999
Michigan Conflict Management Conference, Detroit, November 1998
Association for Counseling and Development National Convention, New York, March 1998
State Substance Abuse Council, Battle Creek, August 1997

District Activities:
Chair, Crisis Intervention Curriculum Project, Wayne County Schools Consortium
Roundtable leader, School/Community Outreach for Youth, Detroit area agencies
Representative, Mayor's Action for Youth Council, King High School
Co-chair, Substance Abuse Prevention Council, Detroit Public Schools
Member, At-Risk Committee for Detroit Area Schools

LEADERSHIP

National Delegate, President's Council on Substance Abuse, 1999
President, Great Lakes Regional Chemical Abuse Association, 1999
Conference Chair, State Crisis Intervention Workshop, Kalamazoo, 1998
Past-President, Michigan Association for Counseling and Development, 1997
Member, Board of Directors, Youth Shelters of Detroit, 1996-present

HONORS and AWARDS

Volunteer of the Year Award, NAACP, 1998   Apple Award Recipient, KRNZ Television, 1997
Blomberg Graduate Assistant Fellowship, 1995   F. J. Scotts Memorial Scholarship, 1995
Dean's List and Presidential Citation   Outstanding Citizen Award, Detroit 1995

PUBLICATIONS

"Crisis Intervention: Everyone Needs to Help," Intervention Newsletter,
        Chicago, Illinois, 5(3), 1999.
"Substance Abuse and Homeless Students," Journal of Substance Abuse,
        Miami, Florida, 8(2), 1999.
"Teenagers-Getting Your Attention the Hard Way," Counselor Education and Supervision,
        2(3), Alexandria, Virginia, Spring 1997.

LICENSURE

National Counselor Certification   State of Michigan Counseling Certification
Private Therapist State Certification   Michigan Secondary Teaching Certificate

KENT LEHTINEN

221 College Street
Any City, State 12345
(101) 555-0009

OBJECTIVE Elementary School Librarian

DEGREES University of Wisconsin-Madison, Madison, Wisconsin
Master of Arts in Library Science, May 2000

Bachelor of Science, August 1995
Elementary Education, Emphasis in Reading

LIBRARY **Practicum**, Central Middle School, Beloit, Wisconsin, November-December 1999
EXPERIENCE **Responsibilities:**
Presented mini-lessons on using library resources to seventh-grade classes
Designed "treasure hunt" skill packets for instruction about library resources
Assisted with selection of print materials
Weeded fiction collection
Planned and developed topical exhibit for the learning resource center
Contributed and assisted with presentation of in-service program for faculty

TEACHING **Classroom Teacher, Grades 3 and 4**, Unity School District, Milltown, Wisconsin, 1996-1999
EXPERIENCE **Responsibilities:**
Taught reading for grades 3 and 4 using whole language concepts
to develop reading and writing skills
Utilized a variety of techniques for instruction in math and science,
with manipulatives and hands-on approaches
Introduced computer skills in the classroom
Co-sponsored summer reading project for all third graders
Committee Assignments:
Writing Process for Elementary Grades
Elementary Computer Committee to implement computer applications
across the curriculum for grades K-6
Outdoor Education Committee
Committee to interview superintendent candidates

ACTIVITIES **Volunteer**, Polk County Library System, 1997-1999
AND INTERESTS **Docent**, Wisconsin State Historical Society, 2000–present
Folktales and Storytelling
Genealogical Research

MEMBERSHIPS American Library Association
American Association of School Librarians
Wisconsin Library Association
Wisconsin Education Association

CREDENTIALS Educational Placement Office
Any City, State 12345-1338   Phone: (101) 555-0008

ANITA REYES

221 College Street, Any City, State 12345   (101) 555-0009

OBJECTIVE

Coordinator of Media Services

EDUCATION

M.L.S. 1993-Instructional Communications Technology
Specialization: School Media Center
University of Vermont, Burlington, Vermont
B.A. 1984-Social Studies Education
Middlebury College, Middlebury, Vermont

AREAS OF EXPERTISE

Computer Assisted Instruction
Computer use in learning resource centers
Evaluation and assessment of instructional materials and software
Curriculum development
In-service programs for K-12 staff development

MEDIA

Media Specialist, Hartford Middle School
White River Junction, Vermont, 1993-present
Responsibilities:
- Establish and maintain learning centers for computer lab
- Consult with teachers on projects and assignments involving computer and multimedia resources
- Evaluate, select, and requisition new software, multimedia, and other print or nonprint materials
- Assist teachers in selection of instructional materials
- Train and supervise media center aides and clerical staff

TEACHING EXPERIENCE

Teacher, Grades 3 and 4, Longfellow Elementary School,
Rosbury, Vermont, 1984-1991
- Team Teacher for social studies, language arts, and science
- Taught individualized math and two reading groups
- Introduced computers into the classroom and taught students to use available software
- Developed and maintained listening and writing centers

RELATED ACTIVITIES

Planning Committee, Vermont Education Association
          Conference on Technology and Instruction (Fall 2001)
Member, Library and Information Technology Association

CREDENTIALS

Career Development Center, Any City, State 12345
(101) 555-0008   FAX: (101) 555-0009

Susie L. Sundberg

221 College Street   Any City, State 12345   (101) 555-0009

DEGREES

M.P.T. Physical Therapy, May 2000, Indiana University, Bloomington

B.A.Biology, May 1998, Wartburg College, Waverly, Iowa *cum laude*

HONORS

Dean's List	Regent's Scholarship, four years
Vicki Klotzbach Scholarship	Elk's Lodge Scholarship

INTERNSHIPS

Orthopedics & Neurology-Outpatient, Gary Medical Center, May-July 1999
Orthopedics-Outpatient, Rock Therapy Center, Moline, July-August 1999
Neurology-Inpatient Rehabilitation Center, Trinity Hospital, Chicago, Fall 1999
    Internship responsibilities include, evaluation, treatment, and progression
    of patient with various diagnoses, discharge planning, collaboration with
    other health care providers, patient and family education, and in-service
    participation.

ADDITIONAL CLINICAL WORK

Participated in clinics at facilities in Iowa in the following areas (1997-2000):
- Orthopedics   - Sports Medicine   - Neurology Rehabilitation
- Pediatrics   - Spine Rehabilitation   - Acute Care
- Wound Care   - Cardiopulmonary   - Home Health Care
    Major responsibilities and experiences included evaluation of patients with
    varied diagnoses, debriding and dressing wounds, assisting and encouraging
    patients with rehablitative exercises and activities, gait training with and
    without assistive devices, monitoring patients during exercise.

RELATED EXPERIENCES

Rehabilitation Aide, Bloomington Medical Center, Fall 1998 to present
Physical Therapy Aide, Mercy Health Center, Dubuque, IA, Summer, 1998
Resident Aide, Development Center, Chicago, Summers 1996 and 1997
Teacher/Advocate/Protector, Prairie House, Hammond, Summer 1996
    Responsibilities in the above positions include:
    - Guided patients through strengthening, balance, and coordination exercises
    - Transported patients to and from therapy sessions
    - Facilitated the learning of ADLs, social skills, educational skills, and vocational
      skills among mentally and physically challenged adults
    - Performed PROM and AAROM exercises with residents

AFFILIATIONS AND ACTIVITIES

Tri Beta, biology honor society
Leadership Workshops and Leadership Mentor/Protégé Program
Biology Mentoring Program, three years
President, Lowden Residence Hall and Peer Review Team
Ace Bowling Volunteer and Wheelchair Challenge Committee member

References Provided Upon Request

ALLISON CORBIN

221 College Street, Any City, State 12345
(101) 555-0009

OBJECTIVE

School Nurse with responsibilities for Grades K-12

EDUCATIONAL BACKGROUND

Bachelor of Science in Nursing, 1999
Alcorn State University, Loman, Mississippi
Associate's Degree in Nursing, 1988
Coahoma Community College, Clarksdale, Mississippi

SELECTED ACADEMIC COURSES

Human Development and Behavior
Nursing Practice in Health Promotion
Health and Cultural Diversity
Psychological Aspects of Adolescence

Human Sexuality
Alcohol and Other Drug Abuse
Self-Help Groups

RECENT PROFESSIONAL DEVELOPMENT WORKSHOPS

Red Cross CPR Trainer Certification
Introduction to American Sign Language
Mandatory Reporting of Child Abuse

Treatment of Eating Disorders
Personal Health Care
Nutrition and Adult-onset Diabetes

EMPLOYMENT EXPERIENCE

Clinic Nurse (part-time), Edgewood Family Practice Clinic, Loman, Mississippi, 1997-
Assist physicians with physical assessments and patient care, manage patient
charts and records, assist in the selection, ordering, and organization of supplies.

Staff Nurse, Mercy Medical Center, Montgomery, Alabama
Pediatric Intensive Care, 1993-1997
Pediatrics, 1990-1993
Obstetrics and Gynecology, 1988-1990

REFERENCES

Available from Teacher Career Center, Any City, State 12345 Telephone: (101) 555-0008

MARTIN EAGLESMITH

221 College Street   Any City, State 12345   (101) 555-0009

EDUCATION

Ed.S. **School Psychology**, 1999, Delta State University, Cleveland, Mississippi

M.A. **Educational Psychology**, 1994, University of Mississippi, University, Mississippi

B.A. **Elementary Education**, 1980, Livingston, Alabama

INTERNSHIP IN SCHOOL PSYCHOLOGY

Washington County School District, Greenville, Mississippi, 1998-1999
Conducted assessments, analyzed data, conducted observations, and reported data
to team members; wrote psychological evaluations.
Member of school multidisciplinary team for identification and programming of
students with special needs.
Wrote goals and objectives to meet individual needs of students, including areas of
substance abuse, social skills training, therapeutic intervention, and parenting.
Consulted with parents and teachers regarding assessment results and problems
related to student's school performance and recommended specific instructional
strategies.

TEACHING EXPERIENCE-17 YEARS

Manning Elementary School, Greenville, Mississippi, 1981-1998
Introduced whole language concept for language arts and reading.
Expanded multicultural curriculum.
Wrote grant to acquire first classroom computer (1982).
Chaired instructional technology committee for elementary teachers at the school.
Developed learning centers for science and mathematics that were adopted throughout
the district.
Taught all elementary subjects except music and art.
Grades 5-6 (5 years); Grade 2 (6 years); Grade 3 (6 years)
Coaching responsibilities included assisting with basketball and track at
Solomon Junior High School and with track and golf at Weston High School.

ACTIVITIES

Coach, Babe Ruth Baseball League, 1982-1997
Volunteer Coordinator, Baseball Fund-raisers-1993-1996
Referee, Western Mississippi High School Football League
Greenville YMCA, executive committee officer for six years
Greenville Area Sunrise Rotary Club, current Past President

CREDENTIALS

Placement file available upon request from Career Planning & Placement Office,
Any City, State 12345. Telephone: (101) 555-0008   FAX: (101) 555-0009

KARIN K. HJELM
221 College Street   Any City, State 12345
(101) 555-0009 (home) (101) 555-1111 (business)

OBJECTIVE:

School Social Worker, K-12

CURRENT PROFESSIONAL EXPERIENCE:

School Social Worker, Lakeland Agency, Madison, Wisconsin, 1998-present
Work as part of an educational team and provide diagnostic, direct, and
consultive services for students in 5 schools and their families.

Family Caseworker, Bureau of Children's Services, Madison, Wisconsin, 1997-1998
Responsible for coordinating home visits of all clients in central Wisconsin;
arranging for medical services and follow-up on financial assistance.

SOCIAL WORK FIELD EXPERIENCES:

School Social Worker, Milwaukee Public Schools, fall semester 1997
Community Liaison, AIDS Coalition, West Chicago, spring semester 1996
Caseworker, Lutheran Social Services, Chicago, summer 1996
Additional three-week internships were completed in hospice,
pediatric AIDS hospital unit, and community mental health.

GRADUATE COURSE CONCENTRATIONS:

Therapy with Children   Cross-Cultural Social Work
Family Dynamics   Working with Groups
Developmentally Disabled   Racism and Discrimination

ACADEMIC TRAINING:

Master of School Social Work   Loyola University of Chicago 1997
                                          Chicago, Illinois
Bachelor of Science-Nursing   University of Evansville 1995
                                          Evansville, Indiana

PROFESSIONAL ASSOCIATIONS:

Academy of Certified Social Workers   National Association of Social Workers
American Public Health Association   Wisconsin Public Health Association

PRESENTATIONS:

"Social Workers as Children's Advocates," major address at the Great Lakes
Association of Social Workers, Gary, Indiana, October 1998.
"Teachers and Social Workers—How to Collaborate," Panel facilitator, Educators'
Conference for Support Services, Chicago, Illinois, Summer 1997.
"Organizing Community Volunteers," Workshop leader, Conference on Volunteers,
Wisconsin United Way Association, Green Bay, Wisconsin, Spring 1996.

References: Furnished Upon Request

MATT PETERSEN

221 College Street, Any City, State 12345 (101) 555-0009 m-petersen@uiowa.edu

DEGREES

M.A.   Speech Pathology and Audiology, 1997-1999, The University of Iowa, Iowa City
Will be qualified to provide speech and language services in hospitals, clinical settings, schools.

B.A.   Mathematics, *with distinction,* 1993-1997, Hamline University, St. Paul, Minnesota

CLINICAL EXPERIENCE

Clinic—Wendell Johnson Speech and Hearing Clinic, 1997-1998, The University of Iowa
Experiences-articulation and voice disorders, cleft palate and aural rehabilitation.
Hospitals—St. Luke's Methodist Hospital, Spring 1998, Cedar Rapids, Iowa
Department of Child Psychology, University of Iowa Hospitals, Spring 1997
Involved remediation of adults with neuropathologies of speech and language and
children with language disorders; also worked with emotionally disturbed children.

PUBLIC SCHOOL EXPERIENCE

Practica: Elementary Speech Services, Penn Elementary School, 1998, North Liberty, Iowa
Preschool Hearing & Language Screening, Wendell Johnson Clinic, 1998
Worked primarily with language-impaired and learning-disabled children.

TRAINING ASSIGNMENTS

Research Assistant, Otolaryngology Department, University of Iowa Hospitals, Spring 1998.
Researched language remediation in emotionally disturbed preschool children.
Co-taught Clinical Procedures with Professor Vera Fine, Fall 1998.
Presented lectures, worked with students, and was responsible for lab evaluations.

PROFESSIONAL SERVICE

Member, American Speech-Language-Hearing Association
President, University of Iowa Speech & Hearing Student Association
Attended American Speech-Language-Hearing Association Convention, Chicago, 1999
Attended Iowa Speech & Hearing Association Meeting, Des Moines, February 1998

ACTIVITIES AND DISTINCTIONS

Dean's List	Elected Graduate College Senator
Phi Kappa Phi	Awarded Millers Foundation Undergraduate Research Grant

COMMUNITY SERVICE

Co-Chair, United Way Fund-raising, University Component, Iowa City, 1998-1999
Member, Citizens for Environmental Action, Eastern Iowa Chapter, 1998-present

References available upon request

KELLY A. DAWSON

221 College Street, Any City, State 12345
Telephone: (101) 555-0009   E-mail: dawson2@bpm.com

EDUCATION:

M.A., Information Sciences, Roosevelt University, Chicago, Illinois, May 2000

B.S., Mathematics, Western Illinois University, Macomb, Illinois, 1994

TECHNOLOGICAL EXPERTISE:

WWW and Internet experience (HTML, CGI scripting, listserv management)
Multimedia experience with Adobe Photoshop, digitizing video and sound
Familiar with Perl, AppleScript and database programming
Knowledge of Novell 4.1, DOS, Windows 3.1, Windows 95, WordPerfect, Microsoft Office
Suites, Lotus Notes, Lotus Mail

TECHNOLOGY EXPERIENCE:

Webmaster and Teaching Assistant, Roosevelt University, 1998-2000
> Taught a graduate course, *Global Networks for Instruction,* for students in the College of Education. Redesigned and maintained the department's WWW site and taught HTML short courses to students and staff. Provided software and hardware support for computer lab consisting of IBM-PCs and Macintosh microcomputers.

Freelance Consultant, September 1997-present
> Experience building Web sites for clients, including design and customization of CGI applications. Taught clients to edit/design their own Web pages. Constructed a flatfile database in FileMaker Pro for compiling student records in the Mathematics Education program at Roosevelt University.

TEACHING EXPERIENCE:

Secondary Mathematics Teacher, Alton High School, Alton, Illinois, 1994-1998
> Taught all mathematics courses for grades 11 and 12, including Advanced Placement Mathematics

Volunteer Mathematics Tutor, Western Illinois University, 1992-1994
> Individual and small group tutoring in mathematics lab

REFERENCES ON FILE:

University Career Development Center, Any City, State 12345 (101) 555-0008

18

ADMINISTRATORS AND SUPERVISORS

ELEANOR FARRELL
221 College Street
Any City, State 12345
(101) 555-0009

INTERESTS AND QUALIFICATIONS

Professional Objective: Assistant Principal
- Experienced facilitator for shared decision-making teams
- Knowledgeable about team approaches, multiage grouping, collaborative learning, and inclusion of ESL students and students with special needs
- Expertise in curriculum including subject integration, whole language, hands-on science, and math manipulatives
- Skilled at involving and communicating with teachers, pupils, and parents

EDUCATION

Master of Education, Elementary School Administration and Supervision, 1998
   Indiana State University, Terre Haute, Indiana
Graduate work (14 hours) in Elementary Education (curriculum) Summers 1993-1995
   Indiana University, Bloomington, Indiana
Bachelor of Science, Elementary Education, 1991
   Bethel College, Mishawaka, Indiana

LICENSURE

Indiana Elementary Administration and Supervision License, grades K-6
Indiana Professional Teaching License, grades K-6

ADMINISTRATIVE INTERNSHIP

Oregon-Davis School Corporation, Hamlet, Indiana, Spring semester 1998
   Oregon-Davis Elementary School, 436 students, 37 certificated staff
- Assist with creation and implementation of student and staff schedules
- Contact and work with parents to improve student behavior and classroom success; for final nine weeks assumed full responsibility, under supervision, for student disciplinary procedures
- Observation and increasing responsibility for staff evaluation, reinforcing quality teaching and fostering improvement
- Work with a software consultant to design and implement a new district technology plan
- Organize and supervise extracurricular events, including student government activities, talent show, community service projects, assemblies, and athletic contests
- Present information to student and parents regarding expectations and programming
- Responsible for editing and production stages of revised student handbook

TEACHING EXPERIENCE

Teacher, Lincoln Elementary School, Peru, Indiana
   Grade 6, 1996-1997;   Grades 3-4, 1991-1996
   • Planned and organized materials for thematic units, with extensive use of
      Reader's Workshop and Writer's Workshop techniques
   • Developed and maintained an active learning environment, including utilization
      of manipulatives in math and science and collaborative learning strategies
   • Initiated parent contacts and conferences to discuss home/school plans to
      enhance student achievement

COMMITTEE RESPONSIBILITIES AND LEADERSHIP

Grade Level Unit Leader   School Improvement Team
Scheduling Committee   District Management Team
Child Study Team   Building Expectations Committee (chair)

PROFESSIONAL DEVELOPMENT

Workshop in Shared Decision Making, July 1996
         Emphasis on team development, strategies for implementation, and facilitation
Conflict Management Seminar, June 1994
         Planning for student/staff training, program evaluation, records maintenance
Conferences Attended:
         New Administrators Conference, 1998
         National Administrators Conference, 1998
         Indiana Conference on At-Risk Students, 1997
         International Reading Association Conferences, 1993-1997
         Young Writers' Conference, Oberlin College, 1996
         Indiana State University Conference on Students with Special Needs, 1996

REFERENCES

Dossier available from Education Careers Office, Any City, State 12345
      Telephone: (101) 555-0008; FAX: (101) 555-0089

H.E. WEN

221 College Street   Any City, State 12345
(101) 555-0009

ADMINISTRATIVE EXPERIENCE

Coordinator of Curricular Change and Staff Development Project, Wheeling, West Virginia, 1997 -
Work directly with twelve county school districts serving more than 55,000 students in Region VI
and with the University of West Virginia to develop strategies for improved instruction in
secondary school mathematics and science, incorporating Scope, Sequence and Coordination
program of the National Science Foundation and consistent with guidelines of the National
Council of Teachers of Mathematics. Develop or coordinate informational and instructional
opportunities for teachers in each district through on-site workshops, in-service, and
telecommunication. Evaluate and assess program components and prepare reports for the
funding agency, National Science Foundation-Systemic Initiative.

University Supervisor, West Virginia University, Morgantown, West Virginia, 1996
Responsible for supervision and evaluation of student teachers in physical sciences; liaison with
cooperating teachers in six school districts.

TEACHING EXPERIENCE

Department Chair (4 years) and Teacher (physics, chemistry, advanced placement chemistry)
Woodrow Wilson High School, Beckley, West Virginia, 1992-1995

Teacher (physical science, physics, and chemistry)
Moorefield High School, Moorefield, West Virginia, 1990-1992

EDUCATION

Ed.D., 1998   Curriculum & Instruction, West Virginia University-Morgantown
*Dissertation: Evaluating the Effectiveness of Science-Technology-
Society Training Programs for Middle School Science Teachers*

M.S., 1993   Chemistry, University of Charleston, Charleston, West Virginia

B.S., 1990   Chemistry, Minor in Mathematics, Frostburg State College, Frostburg, Maryland

SPECIAL RECOGNITION

Distinguished Young Alumni Award, University of Charleston   Fulbright Undergraduate Scholar
Omicron Delta Kappa Upperclass Leadership Honor Society   Presidential Scholar

RECENT PRESENTATIONS

"Planning appropriate biology education in secondary schools." Paper presented at the West Virginia Science Teachers Association Fall Conference, Charleston, West Virginia, October 1999.

"Problem solving in the physical sciences." Workshop for science teachers in Regional Education Service Agency VI, Wheeling, West Virginia, August 1999.

"Scope, sequence, and coordination for secondary science projects." Workshop for science teachers from eleven districts in Regional Educational Service Agency IV, Summersville, West Virginia, April 1998.

Environmental science materials. Paper presented at Maryland Science Teachers Association Spring Conference, Frostburg, April 1998.

Teacher responses to student questions in problem solving. Paper presented at the West Virginia Science Teachers Association Fall Conference, Charleston, West Virginia, October 1997.

COMMITTEE LEADERSHIP

Regional Technology Committee, Chair, Agency IV, 1998-present
Community Relations Council and Advisory Board, Executive Vice President, 1998
Curriculum Change for Science—A Global Perspective, Council Member, 1997-present

PROFESSIONAL MEMBERSHIPS

National Science Supervisors Association

West Virginia Education Association

National Science Teachers Association

West Virginia Science Teachers Association

Association for Supervision & Curriculum Development

PLACEMENT FILE

Career Planning and Placement Any City, State 12345   (101) 555-0008 FAX: (101) 555-0089

WARREN COLSON

221 College Street
Any City, State 12345
(101) 555-0009

PROFESSIONAL OVERVIEW
Athletic Director, 3 years
Head Coach, 7 years
Teacher and Assistant Coach, 5 years

EXPERIENCE
City High School, Santa Fe Public Schools, Santa Fe, New Mexico, 1997-present
Athletic Director and Physical Education Supervisor

Responsibilities include:
- Supervision of a comprehensive physical education curriculum and sports program for all male and female students
- Evaluation and supervision of the physical education and coaching staff
- Organize and schedule interscholastic athletic events
- Prepare and administer the department budget; order and maintain equipment
- Recruit, interview, screen, and recommend for hire potential coaches
- Conduct orientation and in-service education workshops
- Supervise athletic contests and attend appropriate professional meetings

Senior High School, Farmington Public Schools, Farmington, New Mexico, 1992-1996
Head Football Coach

Cibola High School, Yuma Unified High School District, Yuma, Arizona, 1989-1992
Head Football Coach and Head Track Coach

Mountain View Academy, Raton, New Mexico, 1984 - 1989
Business Education Teacher, Physical Education, and Assistant Coach

COACHING HIGHLIGHTS
Named Outstanding Coach of the Year, 1996
Conference Champions, 1991, 1992, and 1996
State Play-off Championship game, second place, 1992
Four players named to All-State teams

PROFESSIONAL AFFILIATIONS
National Association for Sport and Physical Education
New Mexico State Association for Football
State Association for Athletic Administrators
National Education Association

EDUCATIONAL BACKGROUND
New Mexico State University, Las Cruces, New Mexico
B.S. Degree, 1984 Major: Physical Education; Minor: Business Education
M.S. Degree, 1996 Major: Athletic Administration; Emphasis: Management

CREDENTIALS
Placement and Career Services, Any City, State 12345
Telephone: (101) 555-0008 FAX: (101) 555-0089

EILEEN SUTTER-HILL

221 College Street   Any City, State 12345   (101) 555-0009

PROFESSIONAL OBJECTIVE
Coordinator of Early Childhood Family Education Program

SPECIAL TRAINING
- Child development
- Family systems
- Learning environments
- Child learning styles
- Parenting issues
- Cognitive development
- Communications skills
- Early childhood curricula

EDUCATION
Graduate studies in Education and Psychology, 1998-present
Towson State University, Baltimore, Maryland

Bachelor of Science Degree, Major: Psychology, August 1996
Coppin State College, Baltimore, Maryland

Associate Arts Degree, Area of Specialization: Education, 1992-1994
New Community College of Baltimore, Baltimore, Maryland
- Dean's List

TEACHING EXPERIENCE
Early Childhood Educator: Wood Alternative High School, Baltimore, Maryland
1992-present
Responsible for planning and implementing the early childhood education program for parents and children birth-5 years old. Develop and obtain age-appropriate materials for use in the Early Childhood Center. Assist in long-range planning for the total program and participate in outreach and public relations activities. Conduct ongoing parenting sessions for high school parents. Responsibilities also include evaluating the instructional program, which addresses the intellectual, emotional, cultural, social, and physical needs of parents and children in the family education program.

Headstart Preschool Teacher: Willowwind Community Center, Baltimore, Maryland
1988-1990
Taught a wide variety of students ages 3 years to kindergarten. Created and fostered a warm and safe learning environment. Worked closely with parents and encouraged their involvement in all activities.

CIVIC ACTIVITIES
Fund-raiser, Free Medical Clinic, Baltimore, Maryland, 1998-present
Co-director, Crisis Center Food Drive, Baltimore, Maryland 1998-present
Board Member, Baltimore Center for Children with AIDS, 1998-present
Volunteer, Ecumenical Clothing Relief Project, 1998-present

PROFESSIONAL ORGANIZATIONS
National Association for the Education of Young Children
National Coalition Against AIDS
Maryland Association for Alternative Schools

Credentials available at the Career Center
Any City, State 12345 Telephone: (101) 555-0008

JAY KARLSSON
221 College Street Any City, State 12345 (101) 555-0009 (h)

OBJECTIVE:
- Department Chair, Social Studies

SKILLS AND INTERESTS:
- Excellent communication and organizational skills
- Leadership experience and staff evaluation
- Strong background in curriculum development
- Experience in stateside and international settings

TEACHING OVERVIEW:

Stateside: 8 years	Overseas: 4 years
New Trier High School-Wilmette	International School of Stavanger
Broward County Schools-Ft. Lauderdale	Jakarta International School

ACADEMIC BACKGROUND:
Florida International University, Miami, Florida
Ph.D. Global Studies, 1999

University of London, London, England
Fulbright Fellowship in Communication Studies, 1995-1996

Stetson University, Orlando, Florida
Bachelor of Arts Degree in History and English, 1991

Licensure: Florida Administrative License, 7-12; Permanent Teaching Certificate
Teaching Certificate in History and English, State of Illinois

LEADERSHIP EXPERIENCE:
Department Chair, International School of Stavanger, 1998
Responsible for designing master schedule, developing budget
and working closely with individual faculty members.

Faculty Representative to European Council of International Schools
Curriculum Roundtable, London, England, 1996
One of twenty-five representatives who evaluated, discussed, and made
recommendations regarding curricular in international settings.

President, Florida State Council for the Social Studies, 1995
Presided over a 700-member state organization interested in improving
social studies education.

JAY KARLSSON
Page 2

TEACHING EXPERIENCE:
International School of Stavanger, Stavanger, Norway 1995-1997
- History teacher, International Baccalaureate Program

Nova High School, Broward County Schools, Ft. Lauderdale, Florida 1990-1995
- Honors English, American History, Geography

Jakarta International School, Jakarta, Indonesia 1988-1990
- American History I & II, Advanced Placement American History

New Trier Township High School District #203, Wilmette, Illinois 1985-1988
- Composition, English 10, British Literature I

MEMBERSHIPS:
National Council for the Social Studies   Society for History Education
National Council for Teachers of English   Overseas Education Association

GRADUATE ASSISTANTSHIPS:
Teaching Assistant, Social Studies Methods, Florida International, 1998-present.
  Responsibilities include the instruction of two sections of social studies methods
  classes for education majors. Evaluated papers and prepared lectures.
Guest speaker in various classrooms about international education.

International Student Liaison, Global Studies Division, Florida International, 1998
  Assist foreign students with questions or concerns about course requirements,
  scheduling, living arrangements, and campus policies. Help new students cope
  with culture shock and living adjustments in a foreign culture.

SCHOOL SERVICE:
Chair, Extended Learning Program Committee, Stavanger, Norway
Member, Headmaster Interview Committee, Stavanger, Norway
Co-chair, School Improvement Plan Committee, Ft. Lauderdale
Member, Curriculum Enrichment Committee-Humanities, Ft. Lauderdale
In-service Presenter, Humanities in the High Schools, Broward County Schools
Member, Teacher Selection Committee, New Trier High School
Member, English Writing Team (state grant), New Trier High School

CURRENT VOLUNTEER AND RELATED EXPERIENCE:
Guest Speaker, international travel and education topics, Miami, Florida
Volunteer Teacher's Aid, Haitian Refugee Center, Miami, Florida
Adult Tutor, Haitian Community Education Center, North Miami, Florida

References available upon request

KATHLEEN K. JOSEPH
221 College Street Any City, State 12345
(101) 555-0009 kk-joseph@ccbluffs.us

ADMINISTRATIVE STRENGTHS

Human resources management:
- Provide leadership for the planning, coordinating, supervising, and evaluation of all personnel services including recruitment, selection, and assignment of staff.
- Knowledge of state and federal guidelines and legislation (e.g., ADA, Affirmative Action, Civil Rights Act, Age Discrimination) regarding hiring practices and selection procedures.
- Experience in and support for shared decision making and site-based management practices.
- Ability to collaborate and work as a team member with management and the Board of Education, professional and support staff, students, parents, and community.
- Experience with system-wide information management and data-based decision making.

EDUCATIONAL EXPERIENCE SUMMARY

Graduate Research Assistant	The University of Iowa	1999-present
Director of Personnel	Council Bluffs, Iowa	1997-1999
Coordinator of Curriculum & Instruction	Bering Strait, Alaska	1993-1997
Language Arts/Chapter One Coordinator	Avon, Massachusetts	1990-1993
Secondary English Teacher	Agana, Guam	1988-1990

DEGREES

Ph.D.   **Planning, Policy & Leadership Studies**, The University of Iowa, Iowa City, 2000
Dissertation Topic: Analysis of Prescribed Interview Styles and Candidate Ranking

M.A.   **Mass Communication**, Johns Hopkins University, Baltimore, Maryland, 1992
Emphasis: Institutional Public Relations

B.S.   **English and Mass Communication**, University of Guam, Mangilao, Guam, 1988
Phi Beta Kappa   *Graduated with highest distinction*

RECENT SEMINARS AND CONFERENCES

State Leadership Conference, Iowa Association for School Administrators, Des Moines, October 1999
AASPA Symposium on Management Innovations, San Diego, California, July 1999
AASPA National Convention, Leadership Series for Women, Washington, D.C., October 1998
Alaska Association for Bilingual Education, Fairbanks, Alaska, May 1997
Iowa Language Arts Conference (invited speaker), Drake University, Des Moines, May 1996
Northwest Regional States Conference on Outcome Based Education, Seattle, Washington, March 1995

K.K. Joseph
page 2

PROFESSIONAL EXPERIENCE

Director of Personnel, Council Bluffs Community School District, Council Bluffs, Iowa, 8/97-7/99
Planned, developed, and revised personnel management regulations in accordance with Board policy.
Organized effective and appropriate procedures to recruit, select, and retain quality staff.
Monitored the ongoing success of the district's personnel efforts and supervised day-to-day activities.
Implemented a minority recruitment process including the planning of recruitment trips,
compilation of data, screening, interviewing, and maintenance of records.
Developed staffing plans and recommended teaching assignments and district-wide transfers.
Assisted in staff reductions, terminations, and recall proceedings.

Coordinator of Curriculum & Instruction, Bering Strait School District, Unalakleet, Alaska, 1993-1997
- Worked cooperatively with staff and administrators on curriculum issues in 16 villages spanning
 80,000 square miles of rugged terrain.
Facilitated major revision of intermediate curriculum, replacing current programs with integrated
and developmentally appropriate practices.
With staff collaboration, developed a state recognized K-8 literacy program.
Established a business/school partnership to create and equip innovative computer labs.
Designed intensive staff development plan to support curricular change.

Language Arts/Chapter One Coordinator, Avon Public Schools, Avon, Massachusetts, 1990-1993
- Responsibilities included organizing and directing K-12 services in reading and language arts.
 Worked with staff to implement process writing, whole language methodology, reading in the
 content areas, children's literature, alternative assessment, thinking skills infusion, and multiple
 intelligence theory.
- Developed action teams to include staff at all levels.

Secondary English Teacher, Washington High School, Agana, Guam, 1988-1990
 Taught English 9, Honors 10 classes, and Creative Writing, an elective class offered through after-
 school extended learning programs. Advisor of the school newspaper, The Banana Leaf.

GRADUATE ASSISTANTSHIPS

Research Assistant, Institute for School Executives, College of Education, The University of Iowa,
1999-present. Assist with the planning and organization of four major institutes per year. Invite
renowned speakers from across the nation to address school administrators from across the state.
Participated in preparation of a grant funded by the Geraldine Dodge Foundation.

Supervisor of Student Teachers, College of Education, The University of Iowa, 1998-1999.
Responsibilities included supervising, advising, and evaluating thirteen secondary student teachers.
Worked with public school teachers and administrators in a variety of settings. Presented workshops
on classroom management, development of lesson plans, teaching strategies, and salary negotiations.

References provided upon request.

SOFIA BILLERIA

221 College Street   Any City, State 12345
(101) 555-0009
sbilleria@.GTU.edu

EDUCATIONAL EXPERIENCE

Administrative Intern, Central Administrative Office, District of Columbia School District, Fall 1999
- Assisted in all phases of long-range demographic planning for the district. Planning team was led by Associate Superintendent and an urban geographer from Georgetown University.

Research Assistant, Institute for School Administrators, Georgetown University, 1999-present
- Researched and team planned seminar topics for administrators. Topics included technology in education, sexual harassment and school policies, Americans with Disabilities Act, Family Leave Act, blood-borne pathogens literature, and school procedures.

BUILDING LEVEL EXPERIENCE

Assistant Building Principal, grades K-5, Alvord School District, Riverside, California, 1996-1998
- Member of four-member administrative team. Established a positive and orderly climate by opening lines of communication with staff, students, and the community. Encouraged parent involvement and participation in all school events. Worked with team to strengthen staff development program and to increase monies for curriculum writing.

TEACHING EXPERIENCE

Spanish Instructor-Bilingual Teacher-Training Program, University of California-Riverside, 1997-present
Elementary Teacher, grade 4, Mentor Teacher (ESL) American School, El Salvador, 1994-1997
Bilingual Classroom Teacher, grades 2/3, Jurupa United School District, Riverside, California, 1992-1994

EDUCATIONAL BACKGROUND

Master of Arts Degree: Educational Administration, July 2000, Georgetown University, Washington, D.C.
Bachelor of Arts Degree: Elementary-Bilingual Education 1990, California State University, San Bernadino

LICENSURE

Provisional Professional Officer Certificate - District of Columbia, 1999
Professional Credential & Multiple Subjects Credential - State of California; Language Development Specialist Endorsement - State of California

Credentials at Educational Placement Office, Any City, State 12345   Telephone: (101) 555-0008
Portfolio available or visit Web site at: www.sofia.class.htm

Sofia Billeria
page 2

PROFESSIONAL ACTIVITIES AND ACCOMPLISHMENTS

SERVICE AND LEADERSHIP

Committee participation:
- Co-chair, Graduate Student Advisory Committee, 1999-present
- Graduate Student Representative, Five-Year Program Review, 1999
- Chair, English Language Development Committee, 1997
- Vice-Chair, Bilingual Curriculum Committee, 1996-1997
- Member, Student Attendance Review Board, 1996-1997
- Member, Multicultural Curriculum Review Committee, 1995
- Member, Student Study Team, 1995
- Leadership Team Member, Program Quality Review, 1994-1995

In-service presentations:
- Monolingual Teachers and Bilingual Students: How Can We Communicate?
- Cooperative Learning Projects in the Bilingual Classroom
- Understanding Cultural Differences and the ESL Student

Special projects:
- Desert Cities Regional Reading Council
- Strategic Planning Board for Alvord United School District
- Community Parent Outreach Project
- School/Business Alliance of Riverside County

Recent conferences:
- Annual Meeting of the National Association of Elementary School Principals Orlando, Florida, March 1999
- Association of Overseas Educators, Indiana, Pennsylvania, Fall 1998
- Western Regional Meeting of Bilingual Educators, Provo, Utah, Spring 1997

SPECIAL RECOGNITION

Distinguished Teacher of the Year Award, California State University
Georgetown University Graduate Thesis Award for Outstanding Research
Graduate Leadership Award, College of Education, Georgetown University
Undergraduate Achievement Scholarship, California State University

PROFESSIONAL AFFILIATIONS

National Association of Elementary School Principals   Association of Overseas Educators
Association for Supervision and Curriculum Development   California Women in Educational Leadership

David M. Logarmancia
221 College Street Any City, State 12345
(101) 555-0009 (home) (101) 555-0089 (office)

OBJECTIVE AND INTERESTS:

High School Principal
- Encourage parent involvement and participation in school
- Communicate effectively and build collaborative ties between school and community members and organizations
- Skilled in site-based management
- Accessible to all constituents

EDUCATION:

M.S. Educational Administration - May 1997 Point Park College, Pittsburgh
Thesis: "Personnel Selection Factors: Criteria & Process for Screening"
B.S. Degree, Physics, 1990 *summa cum laude*

Claremont Graduate School, Claremont, California
Scholar-in-Residence Summer Program, 1998
Topic: Educational Administration in Urban Schools

ADMINISTRATIVE EXPERIENCE:

High School Assistant Principal, Oliver High School, Pittsburgh, Pennsylvania
Major responsibilities 1997-present:
- Direct responsibility for the supervision of the computerized management system including grade reporting, attendance, and records.
- Responsible for student disciplinary procedures for fifty percent of the student body; also included follow-up and parental conferences.
- Conducted performance evaluations of the science and math faculty members.
- Supervised day-to-day instructional budget operations.
- Worked closely with the Allegheny County Sheriff's Liaison Program.
- Involved with the Pittsburgh Center for Alcohol and Drug Services.

TEACHING EXPERIENCE:

Physics Teacher, Oliver High School, Pittsburgh, Pennsylvania, 1987-1990
- Taught Physics, Science Research, and AP Physics
- Advisor to Science Club and Chair of Pennsylvania Space Fair

ACTIVITIES AND AFFILIATIONS:

- Strategic Planning Action Team Member and Facilitator, 1998-
- Negotiation Team Member for Pittsburgh Administrators' Association, 1998
- NCA Steering Evaluation Committee Member, Oliver High School, 1996
- Pittsburgh New Schools Development Corporation Regional Member, 1995-
- Co-chair, Site-based Management Committee, 1994-1995
- President, Pittsburgh Science Association, 1994
- National Association of Secondary School Principals
- School Administrators of Pennsylvania

CREDENTIALS

Teacher Career Center   Any City, State 12345 (101) 555-0008

BARBARA KLEIN

221 College Street
Any City, State 12345
(101) 555-0009

PROFESSIONAL OVERVIEW
- Special Education Consultant   3 years
- Education Prescriptionist   4 years
- Special Education Teacher   5 years
- Behavior Management Specialist   2 years

COMPETENCIES

Special Education Supervision   Compliance Monitoring
In-service Training   Psycho-educational Testing
Collaborative Consultation   Diagnostic-Prescriptive Teaching

CONSULTING AND SUPERVISORY EXPERIENCE
Educational Service Unit 31, Cheney, Washington, 1998 - present
Behavior Disorder Specialist and General Special Education Consultant

Department of Defense Dependents Schools, Munich, Germany, 1994 - 1998
Educational Prescriptionist

Mississippi Bend Area Educational Agency, Bettendorf, Iowa, 1992 - 1994
Special Education Consultant

Responsibilities in the above positions included:
- Supervision of special education programs pre-K - 12 grades
- Consulting with parents, administrators, teachers, and referral agencies
- Coordination with state and local programs in designing projects and writing grants
- Providing assistance in curricula, program, IEP development, and pre-intervention
- Assisting schools in compliance with federal and state special education regulations
- Furnishing in-service training programs to parents, schools, and outside agencies
- Giving psycho-educational testing and participating in interdisciplinary team staffings
- Training staff in techniques for dealing with behavior problem students

CLASSROOM EXPERIENCE
International School of Helsinki, Helsinki, Finland, 1990 - 1992
Behavior Disorders and Learning Disabilities Teacher
Senior Class Advisor; Sophomore Girl's Basketball Coach

Cooperative Education Service Unit, Elm Grove, Wisconsin, 1986 - 1990
Secondary Special Education Multi-disability Resource Teacher
Faculty Advisor to Students Against Drunk Driving Club

Kauai School District, Waimea, Kauai, 1984 - 1986
Behavior Specialist and In-school Suspension Teacher
Intramural Director

PROFESSIONAL AFFILIATIONS
Association for Overseas Educators
American Association for Curriculum and Development
Washington Association for Exceptional Children
National Association of Supervisors and Directors of Secondary Education

BARBARA KLEIN
page 2

EDUCATIONAL BACKGROUND
University of Hawaii-Manoa, Honolulu, Hawaii
Bachelor of Science Degree, 1979 Major: Special Education (K - 12)
Master of Arts Degree, 1990 Behavior Disorders

Additional special education graduate course work completed at:
University of Washington, Seattle
Michigan State University - Summer Campus, Cyprus
Iowa State University, Ames

LICENSURE
Minnesota dual licensure in Emotional/Behavior Disabilities and Learning Disabilities
Iowa and Washington Supervisory (K-12) Special Education Certificates
Washington licensure in Emotional/Behavior, Learning Disabled, and General
Special Education

CURRENT PROFESSIONAL ACTIVITIES
<u>Training sessions:</u>
"Orientation Programs and New Staff Success," staff training sessions presented at six
regional centers in Oregon and Washington, 1998 - present

"Quality Assurance/Peer Review Programs," supervisory training sessions offered for referral
agencies and special education service units in Washington, 1997 - 1998

"Understanding and Monitoring Rules and Regulations with Third Party Systems," in-house
training sessions for directors of various departments, Cheney, Washington, 1997 - 1998

<u>Committees:</u>
Chair, Northwest Regional Special Education Staff Consortium
Chair, Orientation Review Committee, Educational Service Unit I
Member, Computerized Special Education Resources Inventory System

TRAVEL AND INTERNATIONAL INTERESTS
- Travels in England, Germany, France, Switzerland, Italy,
  Cyprus, Jordan, Egypt, Kenya, Morocco, Spain, and China
- Co-founder, ASIA Outreach Program, Cheney, Washington
- Host Family, Foreign Field Service Students
- Member, International Woman's Club
- Volunteer, Americares Association

MILITARY SERVICE
United States Air Force, Second Lieutenant - Air Borne Division, 1979 - 1983
Awarded commendations for flight training and flight performance, 3 years

CREDENTIALS
Education Placement Office, Any City, State 12345
Telephone: (101) 555-0008 FAX: (101) 555-0089

BROOK LEE GREYLAND

221 College Street, Any City, State 12345   (101) 555-0009   (909) 333-0003 (office)

INTERESTS AND SKILLS

Staff Development and In-service Training   Curriculum Development/Leadership
Technology and Business Partnerships   Bilingual/Multicultural Expertise

CURRENT PROFESSIONAL RESPONSIBILITIES

Administration:

Principal, Thermopolis Middle School, Thermopolis, Wyoming, 1997-present

▶Responsible for administration of a staff of 128 teachers; student body of 1420.

▶Promoted extensive technology infusion into teaching and administrative routines.

▶Co-led a business partnership initiative with Wyoming business leaders to fund technology
  purchases in district. LAN network installed with both Macintosh and Windows environment.

▶Extensive teacher training in software applications. Involved parents in evening technology
  sessions and initiated a parent advisory committee.

▶Created a weekly newsletter to improve communication with parents.

▶Chaired local continuing education committee and worked closely with community leaders
  on a continuing basis.

Consultant:

Private educational consultant, 1996-present

▶Present in-service programs on technology for various audiences both educational and business

▶Develop tailored programs for school districts initiating special programs

▶Speak at regional and national seminars and conferences

EDUCATIONAL EXPERIENCE

Assistant Principal, Rawlins High School, Rawlins, Wyoming, 1994-1996
   Duties included discipline, attendance, behavioral conferences, and class and staff scheduling.
Head Counselor, Wyoming Girls' School, Sheridan, Wyoming, 1992-1994
Counselor and Family Living Teacher, Sheridan, Wyoming, 1990-1992

ACADEMIC TRAINING

Ed.S. Educational Administration, University of Wyoming, 1996
M.A. Counseling, University of Wyoming, 1990
B.S.   Home Economics, University of Maine-Orono, 1987

PROFESSIONAL MEMBERSHIPS

Women in Educational Leadership   National Association of Secondary School Principals
Friends of Foreign Students   American School Counselors Association

LANGUAGE AND TRAVEL

Bilingual - Spanish; traveled extensively in Mexico, Central and South America

—References and additional professional information available upon request—

155

MELANIE HAYES

221 College Street   Any City, State 12345   (101) 555-0009

DEGREES

Ph.D. Educational Administration, August 1998
Syracuse University, Syracuse, New York
Dissertation: History of Pre-service Training: Success and Failure of New Teachers

Master of Arts Degree, Educational Policy, June 1992
Trenton State College, Trenton, New Jersey
 • Graduate Fellow

Master of Arts Degree, Music Education, May 1986
Queens College-City University of New York, New York

Bachelor of Music Degree, Major: Theory, August 1984
Eastman School of Music, Rochester, New York

PROFESSIONAL EXPERIENCE SUMMARY

 • **Superintendent of Schools**, Westhill Schools, Syracuse, New York, 1996 - present
 • **Assistant Superintendent for Curriculum and Instruction**, Upper Township Schools, Tuckahoe, New Jersey, 1992 - 1996
 • **Principal**, Upper Township Middle School, Tuckahoe, New Jersey, 1991 - 1994
 • **Assistant Principal**, Fleming Middle School, Trenton, New Jersey, 1988 - 1991
 • **Vocal Music Teacher**, PS #50 Talfourd Lawn School, Queens District #28 Jamaica, New York, 1985 - 1988
 • **Singer**, New York City Clubs, 1984 - 1985

CIVIC ACTIVITIES

President, Northside Repertory Company, 1998
Board Member, Syracuse American Red Cross Chapter, 1998 - present
Co-director, Chamber of Commerce Leadership Series, 1998 - present
Board Member, Friends of the Syracuse Public Library, 1997 - 1998
Volunteer Director, City Girls' Choir and Performing Troupe, 1996 - 1998

RECOGNITION

Awarded Certificate of Merit, New York Music Teachers' Association
Awarded Outstanding Doctoral Student Scholarship by Syracuse University
Named New Jersey Middle School Principal of the Year, 1994
Listed in *Who's Who in Education*

PROFESSIONAL ORGANIZATIONS

National Association of Secondary Principals
American Association of School Administrators
Association for Supervision and Curriculum Development

CURRENT PROFESSIONAL SERVICE

Chair, Steering Committee, Performance-based Compensation
Chair, Committee for Education Extended Beyond the Classroom
Board Member, School Administrators of New York
Representative, Governor's Commission on New Schools
President, State Women's Caucus for Administrators

Complete list of publications and presentations available upon request

19

NONCERTIFIED TEACHERS

DEAN HUGHES
221 College Street
Any City, State 12345
(101) 555-0009

TEACHING COMPETENCIES

Painting	Printmaking	Ceramics
Drawing	Design	Sculpture

TEACHING EXPERIENCE

Teacher Incentive Program (TIP), Kentucky Arts Council, 1998-1999
> In collaboration with teachers in Kentucky schools, developed projects to enhance visual arts instruction. Designed and implemented innovative projects, including thirteen residencies ranging from one to three weeks, with emphasis on printmaking, painting, and collage. As artist-in-residence, worked directly with students of all ages, kindergarten through high school.

Art Instructor, Louisville Art Guild, Louisville, Kentucky, 1998
> Taught weekly evening classes for adults in drawing, painting (oils, acrylics, watercolor), and woodcuts. Saturday morning classes for children, including instruction in drawing and ceramics.

Teaching Assistant, University of Kentucky, Louisville, Kentucky, 1996-1998
> Responsible for instruction and supervision of lithography studio for undergraduate art majors.

EXHIBITIONS

Juried Shows:
> Purchase Prize, 46th Annual Artists Showcase, Louisville Public Library, 1998
> Invitational, Wimsee Art Center, Knoxville, Kentucky, 1998
> Honorable Mention, Louisville Annual Art in the Park Celebration, 1997

Solo Exhibits:
> Louisville Art Association, 1998
> University of Kentucky DeWare Gallery, 1998
> Avenue C Gallery, Louisville, Kentucky, 1997

EDUCATION

M.F.A. 1998   Printmaking, University of Kentucky, Louisville, Kentucky

B.A.   1995   Art and Art History, Winthrop College, Rock Hill, South Carolina

REFERENCES

Emma Sue Pervisor	Annie Person	Art DeLer
Kentucky Arts Council	Louisville Art Guild	Avenue C Gallery
(101) 555-0101	(101) 555-0102	(101) 555-0100

JUNE ENGLUND
221 College Street
Any City, State 12345
(101) 555-1111

OBJECTIVE
Professional position in a multicultural environment.

SPECIAL SKILLS
- Able to work with people of diverse backgrounds and skill levels.
- Skilled in program development, behavior strategies, and staff management.
- Open-minded, flexible, patient, and a cooperative team member.
- Speak Spanish; knowledgeable about cultural differences.

EDUCATION
Graduate Studies in Psychology, Rollins College, Winter Park, Florida, 1997 - present
B.A. Psychology and Religion, Palm Beach Atlantic College, West Palm Beach, Florida, 1994

TEACHING EXPERIENCE
Kindergarten Teacher, South Miami Lutheran School, Miami, Florida, 1998 - present.
- Plan, instruct, and evaluate kindergartners' cognitive, social, gross, and fine motor development using self-prepared lesson plans.
- Prepare lessons that emphasized cooperative and multicultural learning.
- Use creativity and variety to interest students in classroom activities.
- Maintain frequent parental contact through conferences, telephone conversations and weekly newsletters.

Migrant Head Start Supervisor, Broward County Migrant Child and Family Services, Davie, Florida, 1996–1998.
- Organized the child care needs, health, and education of preschool children of migrant agricultural workers.
- Worked with teachers in full-day and extended-day programs in nine different centers.
- Collaborated with health professionals who addressed the daily and ongoing health needs of the children.

Assistant Director and Preschool Teacher, Mercy Child Development Center, Pensacola, Florida, 1994–1996.
- Developed and implemented summer school enrichment program.
- Supervised staff, trained new teachers, conducted staff meetings, and developed budget.
- Taught four year olds in pre-kindergarten classroom.

VOLUNTEER ACTIVITIES
Volunteer reader, Hear Me Read Program, Miami Public Library
Program Chair, Teenage Parents' Retreat, YWCA, West Palm Beach
Friends Youth Program, Longmont State Mental Hospital, Pensacola

PROFESSIONAL SERVICE
Board Member, Florida Migrant Education Council, Tallahassee, 1999 - present
Presenter, Child Care Conference of Southern Florida, Miami, October 1999
Conference Chair, Florida Conference on Migrant Education, Ft. Lauderdale, Fall 1998
Key address, Governor's Conference on Migrant Education, Tallahassee, Spring 1998
Co-author, *Child Care on the Move*, staff manual prepared for Migrant Family Services, 1998

References provided upon request.

LINDA HASLER

221 College Street
Any City, State 12345
(101) 555-0009

OBJECTIVE:
French or German teacher in a private setting.
Extracurricular interests in crew and language clubs.

EDUCATION:
Teacher Training Course, The Shady Hill School
Cambridge, Massachusetts, 1998–1999
(Post-graduate year of apprenticeship in teaching)

Yale University, New Haven, Connecticut
Bachelor of Arts Degree - May 1998
    Majors: French and German
    with distinction and honor

Institute of European Studies, Nantes, France
Program in French language and culture, 1994

TEACHING
APPRENTICE:
Apprentice Language Teacher, The Shady Hill School
    Cambridge Massachusetts, School year, 1998–1999

Responsibilities:
- Taught French classes, levels I, II and III, and beginning German under the tutelage of the Directing Teacher
- Used various teaching techniques to allow for differing learning styles
- Provided tutorial services for students needing additional help
- Evaluated student progress and held regular student conferences
- Monitored language lab and assisted students with computer software
- Observed and participated in numerous workshops, seminars, and conferences throughout the year
- Organized, in conjunction with the History Department, a Cultural Fair highlighting language, customs, and historical perspectives

RELATED
EXPERIENCES:
Senior Counselor, Concordia Language Villages, Moorhead, Minnesota
Summer 1998
Responsibilities:
- Taught French language skills to villagers of all ages
- Organized and led large and small group activities
- Maintained a high energy level while dealing with repetition
- Related to villagers on a personal level as a teacher and a counselor

YWCA Counselor, Minnetonka Day Camp, Minnetonka, Minnesota
Summer 1997
Responsibilities:
- Taught nature lore and environmental awareness units
- Coordinated day-long canoe trips for campers in all age groups

School Bus Driver, Cambridge Coach Company, New Haven, Connecticut
Summer school sessions and part-time, 1996–1997
Responsibilities:
- Interacted effectively with students, parents, and school staff
- Maintained discipline under adverse conditions

ACTIVITIES:
- Coxswain, Yale Crew Team, 3 years
- Elected Captain of the Yale Crew Team, 1998
- Advanced to crew national competition (6th place)
- Member, New Haven Chapter, United Nations Organization
- Volunteer, Host Family Volunteers - International Student Association
- Treasurer, International Dormitory

AWARDS:
Recontres Internationales de Jeunes a Avignon (achievement scholarship) 1998
Honors House Member, 1996–1998
National Merit Scholar, 1995

TRAVEL:
France, Germany, England, Netherlands, and Greece
*Lived with a French family in 1997. Traveled and visited
museums, cathedrals, and historical sites in all countries.*

LANGUAGES:
Excellent command of French and German (near native fluency)
Moderate abilities in Spanish and Greek

INTERESTS:
Sailing, philately, and wilderness expeditions

**CREDENTIALS
ON FILE:**
Career Planning and Placement Center
Any City, State 12345 (101) 555-0008

GEORGE TALABIAN
221 College Street
Any City, State 12345
Phone: (101) 555-0009
E-MAIL: TALABIAN@HUBACS.BITNET

OBJECTIVE:

Classroom teacher: History
Extracurricular: Sponsor for Academic Decathlon, Knowledge Bowl, and Model United Nations; Rugby Coach

EDUCATION:

Hofstra University, Hempstead, New York
Ph.D. European History - May 2000
Comprehensive Areas: Medieval Europe,
Europe (1500-1815) and Women in Early Societies

Kings College, Cambridge University, Cambridge, England
Medieval Studies - 1997

State University of New York at Albany, Albany, New York
M.A. Renaissance History - 1995   B.A. History and Art - 1993

The Haverford School, Haverford, Pennsylvania
Diploma *with honors* - 1990

RELATED EXPERIENCE:

Teaching Assistant, History Department, Hofstra University, 1999-
Responsibilities include instruction and grading of a two-semester course, Economic and Social History of Medieval Europe. Organized extra study and review sessions; maintained regular office hours to assist students.

Academic Tutor, Athletic Department, Hofstra University, 1998-
Responsibilities included working individually with athletes who needed assistance with research papers and test preparation.

PEACE CORPS:

Community Development, Arish, Yemen, 1995 and 1996
Worked with several village leaders to develop water delivery systems and improve the quality of drinking water

ACTIVITIES AND AWARDS:

- United Nations Graduate Intern Fellowship, Summer 1999
- Representative, Graduate Student Senate, 1996
- Member, American Historical Association
- Member, Renaissance Society of America
- John T. McMellon History Award, 1996
- Presidential Scholar, 1990-1993

CREDENTIALS ON FILE:

University Placement Service
Any City, State 12345 (101) 555-0008

Alan J. Harney

Interdisciplinary Humanities

221 College Street, Any City, State 12345   (101) 555-0009   ajharney@nwu.edu

- Academic background in Greek and Latin, English, and Philosophy
- Training as a teaching assistant at university level
- Good command of French; reading comprehension in German and Italian

Education:

B.A. Classics, 1988
Lake Forest College
Lake Forest, Illinois

M.A., Expository Writing, 1994
Duke University
Durham, North Carolina

M.A., Classics, 1992
Drake University
Des Moines, Iowa

Ph.D., Comparative Literary Studies
(in progress)
Northwestern University
Evanston, Illinois

Teaching experience:

Department of English, Northwestern University, 1999-
  Graduate instructor for undergraduate composition course (2 semesters).
  Teaching assistant for undergraduate course in Renaissance Literature
  (2 semesters) and survey course in World Literature.

Harold Washington College, City Colleges of Chicago, Chicago, Illinois, 1997-1998
  Instructor, Writing Laboratory. Individual and small-group instruction. Worked
  with students at various levels of proficiency; students may seek assistance
  from the Writing Lab voluntarily or by faculty referral.

Department of Classics, Drake University, Des Moines, Iowa, 1995-1996
  Visiting Instructor for introductory classes in Latin; taught one upper-level
  course in Greek mythology; Interim course (3-weeks) in Greek comedy.

Department of Classics, Drake University, 1991-1992
  Teaching assistant for Latin I and II (2 semesters each).

Additional professional activities:

Assistant Editor, *Classics Review,* departmental publication at Drake University
Student representative to departmental review committee, Northwestern University

Awards:

Paulinus Scholarship (for first-year of graduate study)
Andrew Bellingham Ward Fellowship for thesis research

References Available Upon Request

JENNIFER DEANE
221 College Street
Any City, State 12345
(101) 555-0009

STRENGTHS

Early childhood program expertise in:
- Positive Image Development   - Social Relations
- Writing & Language Skills   - Cognitive Development

PRESCHOOL EXPERIENCE

Kinderhaven Preschool, Eureka, California, 1999-
Teacher, Ages 3-5; Responsibilities include:
- Planning, implementing, assessing curriculum with emphasis on developmentally appropriate activities
- Establishing learning/activity centers with using manipulatives
- Creating and maintaining an environment that allows and encourages children to make discoveries, solve problems, and think independently
- Evaluate children's progress through ongoing observation and assessment of cognitive, social, and motor development
- Maintaining frequent parental contact through conferences, telephone conversations, and regular newsletters
- Participating in monthly meetings of the school's Board of Directors and in all school functions including fund-raising

RELATED EXPERIENCE

Claremont Elementary School, Chico, California, 1988-1992
Teacher Associate
- Assisted two teachers with classroom activities for all-day kindergarten classes, including students with special needs

EDUCATION

California State University, Chico, California
B.S. Early Childhood Education (in progress)

California State University, Chico, California
B.A. Psychology, 1988

College of the Sequoias, Visalia, California
A. A. Child Development, 1984

PROFESSIONAL DEVELOPMENT

Recent professional seminars include:
Chico Area Early Childhood Conference, June 2000
Health and Safety Issues for Children, March 2000
Psychology of the Young Child, November 1999
Mandatory Child Abuse Reporting Seminar, May 1999

REFERENCES

Available upon request

TINA KIRKLAND

221 College Street   Any City, State 12345
(101) 555-1111

PROFESSIONAL INTERESTS
- Working with adolescent students in a private setting
- Advising and counseling students with academic or personal concerns
- Developing educational, recreational, and social programming for residence hall life
- Familiar and skilled in various technology/multimedia applications

ACADEMIC BACKGROUND
School for International Training, Brattleboro, Vermont,   June 2000
M.A. Counseling and Human Development   Emphasis: Student Personnel

Norwich University, Northfield, Vermont, . May 1995
B.A. Economics and English

Hotchkiss School, Lakeville, Connecticut,   May 1992
Diploma with Honors

EXPERIENCE
Graduate Assistant-Student Affairs, Division of Housing, School for International Training, 1999 - present
Assisted in the advising and supervision of eight student staff members in two separate units of 600 students. Responsible for implementation of administration policies, personal/academic concerns of residents.

Hall Coordinator, Department of Residence Services, The University of Maine, 1998 - 1999
Responsible for the overall organization, administration, and supervision of a coed undergraduate hall of 400 students. Selected, trained, and evaluated a staff consisting of seven resident assistants and four clerical staff. Specific duties encompassed facility management, counseling, discipline, and advising hall government.

Resident Advisor and Instructor, Cranbrook Schools, Bloomfield Hills, Michigan, August 1995 - 1997
Responsibilities included advising and counseling students with academic or personal concerns; intervening in crisis and conflict situations and coordinating the educational, recreational, and social programming of a 370-member residence hall. Teaching duties included senior level Economics and sophomore Composition. Maintained close communication with faculty and administration concerning student progress.

Tutor, Hartford Public Schools Summer Reading Program, Hartford, Connecticut, 1994 and 1995
Worked with individual students to maintain their current reading level or to develop new strategies in learning to read. Worked with diverse students in an inner-city setting.

ACTIVITIES AND AFFILIATIONS
International Partner Program, member and staff volunteer, Office of International Affairs, Brattleboro, 1999
Volunteer Teacher, International Preschool and Tutoring Center for University Students, Brattleboro, 1999
Resident Assistant, North Towers Dormitories, Norwich University, Northfield, Vermont, 1994 - 1995
Lived in Jordan and Saudi Arabia - attended international schools from 1988 - 1990
Active membership: Michigan Student Personnel Association, American College Personnel Association; American Association for Counseling and Development

References provided upon request.

BRIAN MAX

221 College Street
Any City, State 12345
(101) 555-0009

PROFESSIONAL EXPERIENCE

Abington Friends School, Jenkintown, Pennsylvania, 1995 - present
Skills Lab Instructor, grades 9-12
Work with individual students in all academic areas. Determine needs of students and supplement with appropriate learning materials. Coordinate with teachers the best approach for students' academic success. Expanded skills lab to include computer-aided instruction, electronic bulletin boards, and written materials appropriate for all skill levels.

Team Leader, Mexico Work Camp, May - July, 1999
Chaperoned 15 students on a work camp trip to central Mexico. Lived in a rural area with local families and assisted in field work, village building projects, road maintenance, and child care.

INTERNSHIP

Friends Academy, North Dartmouth, Massachusetts, August 1994 - May 1995
Food Service Intern
Assisted Food Coordinator in planning and producing nourishing and appealing meals for students and staff. Food choices involved meat, vegetarian dishes, and vegan dishes. Worked mostly in evenings and weekends. Supervised and instructed students interested or assigned to food preparation. Intern responsibilities also included living in the dormitory and assuming daily duties.

RELATED ACTIVITIES

- Traveled with students on work trips to Belize, Jamaica, Haiti, and Mexico
- Studied "Landfill Archaeology" at the University of Arizona, Summer 1998
- Attended Yale Summer Institute on the Rebirth of Classics for Secondary Students
- Facilitator for panel discussion on *Academic Success of Boarding School Students from Foreign Countries* at Independent Educational Services Conference, San Francisco

WORK EXPERIENCE

Night shift Chef, Hamburg Inn, Canton, Ohio, June 1995 - December 1995
Assistant Night Manager, McDonalds, Canton, Ohio, 1992 - 1994
Line Server, Dettermine Dormitory, Malone College, 1991 - 1992

EDUCATIONAL BACKGROUND

Malone College, Canton, Ohio
    Bachelor of Arts Degree, 1990 - 1995
    Majors: Archaeology, Philosophy and Latin

Friends Academy, Locust Valley, New York
    High School Diploma, 1990
    Friends' Scholar Distinction
    National Merit Scholar

REFERENCES

Dr. Ed Master, Abington Friends School, (101) 555-0101
Mr. Abel Mentor, Dean of Students, Malone College, (101) 555-0102

ELIZABETH DAVIS
221 College Street
Any City, State 12345
(101) 555-0009

INTERESTS
Theatre Instructor and Technical Director

TEACHING EXPERIENCE
Mankato State University, Mankato, Minnesota, 1990–1992
Teaching Assistant. Responsible for laboratory courses, teaching appropriate techniques and evaluating student projects and performance. Supervised production crews in set construction, stagecraft, lighting, and sound.

RELATED EXPERIENCE
Technical Director, Designer, and Production Coordinator, for eight high school dramatic productions and three musicals, at St. Agnes High School, Academy of the Holy Angels, and DeLasalle High School (Twin City area schools). Taught stagecraft skills to high school students and supervised student production crews (1994-1997).

PROFESSIONAL EXPERIENCE
Chimera Theatre, St. Paul, Minnesota, 1996-present
Production manager, responsible for recruiting technicians, including volunteers, coordinating all technical crews, maintaining production schedules, and overseeing production budgets.

Old Log Theatre, Excelsior, Minnesota, 1993-1995
Technician, with responsibilities in lighting, sound, and rigging; **Lighting Designer**, twelve productions, **Sound Designer**, eight productions, **Set Designer**, three productions.

Paul Bunyan Playhouse, Bemidji, Minnesota, Summers 1990-1993
Various technical responsibilities in set construction, stagecraft, lighting, and sound; **assistant stage manager** for two productions, 1992; **stage manager** for three productions, 1993.

Complete list of production credits available on request.

EDUCATION
Mankato State University, Mankato, Minnesota
M.A. Theatre Arts, 1992
College of St. Catherine, St. Paul, Minnesota
B.A. Speech Communication and Drama, 1990

REFERENCES
Available upon request

20

INTERNATIONAL SETTINGS

NATHANIEL HAGEDORN

221 College Street, Any City, State 12345   (101) 555-0009

OBJECTIVE

Administrator—International Schools
- 8 years of combined administrative K-12 experience
- strong background in curriculum development, technology, and finance
- executive management and organizational skills

EDUCATION

Ph.D. Educational Administration, 1996, University of Idaho, Moscow, Idaho
M.A. Secondary Curriculum/Administration, 1988, University of Utah, Salt Lake City
B.S. Mathematics and Biology, 1985, McKendree College, Lebanon, Illinois
International Study, Oxford, England

ADMINISTRATIVE EXPERIENCE

- Assistant Superintendent, 1996 - present, Independent Schools #21, Lewiston, Idaho
K-12 enrollment of 21,076, instructional staff of 372, nonteaching staff of 229. Sixty-two percent of graduating seniors attend postsecondary institutions. Developed teaching partnership with International School in Rabat with teacher exchanges every two years, student exchange semesters every three years. Current initiatives include technology integration for individual classrooms with intensive staff training sessions, professional staff development, and site-based management.

Previous positions:
- High School Principal and Curriculum Director, 1994-1996, District #29, Rich, Utah
- Assistant Principal, 1991-1993, West Chicago High School, West Chicago, Illinois

TEACHING EXPERIENCE

- The American School of Barcelona, Barcelona, Spain, secondary mathematics, 1988-1991
- Aledo Community School District 217, Aledo, Illinois, mathematics and debate, 1984-1987

LANGUAGES, TRAVEL, AND STUDY

Extensive travel in Spain, France, Italy, Greece, North Africa.
Good comprehension and speaking ability in Spanish, reading knowledge of French.
Studied at Oxford in 1997 and University of London as an undergraduate.

CURRENT CIVIC ACTIVITIES

Board member, Clay United Way, 1999 -   Founding member, Conservation Project, 1997
President, Meadows Youth Service, 1998 -   Chair, Youth Homes, Inc., West Chicago, 1996

OTHER RELEVANT INFORMATION

Memberships-Idaho ASA; AASA; AAIE
Married; spouse elementary teacher; two daughters, ages 14 and 11; U.S. citizen

Complete résumé including conference presentations and publications available for review upon request. Dossier available from Career Planning and Placement, Any City, State 12345

REGGIE S. SUMMIT

221 College Street   Any City, State 12345
(101) 555-0009 (home) (101) 545-0005 (school)

PROFESSIONAL SKILLS AND INTERESTS:
- Experience in leadership roles at the department, building, and district level
- Working with international students and staff in a collaborative setting
- Teaching International Baccalaureate and Advanced Placement courses
- Working closely with expatriate families whose children will attend U.S. colleges

TEACHING EXPERIENCE:
Teacher and Department Chair, Social Sciences, Henry High School
    San Diego Unified School District, San Diego, 1997-present
History and Advanced European History Teacher, Wilcox High School
    Santa Clara Unified School District, Santa Clara, 1992-1995

EXPERIENCE HIGHLIGHTS:
Participated in California Collaborative Teacher Intensive Training Program
Conducted new teacher performance evaluations and tenure review sessions
Developed collaborative teaching projects among English and history faculty
Received state educational grant for advanced placement course training
Directed the statewide Advanced Placement European History Curriculum Project
Editor for a national newsletter for advanced placement history teachers

CURRENT COMMITTEE LEADERSHIP:
Member, California Committee for Talented and Gifted High School Students
Chair, San Diego Social Studies Curriculum Revision Project
Faculty Representative, Superintendent's Parent Advisory Board
Regional Consortium Delegate, State Department of Public Education 2000

PROFESSIONAL MEMBERSHIPS:
ASCD and NEA   Society for History Education
Council for European Studies   American Historical Association

ACADEMIC BACKGROUND:
Stanford University, Stanford, California
    M.A. Medieval History (1997)   Ph.D. Curriculum and Instruction (1998-present)
Santa Clara State University, B.A. European History and Middle Eastern Studies (1992)

SPECIAL RECOGNITION (1997-):
Commencement Speaker (chosen by senior class) three years
Governor's Award for Outstanding Work with Talented and Gifted, 1999
Appointed to President's Council on Learning, 1998
Outstanding Teacher Award, Stanford University, 1997
Selected for United Nations Middle East Study Trip, 1997

References available upon request.

ERIN FRIENDE

| 21 College Street | Any City, State 12345 | (101) 545-0009 |

SKILLS AND INTERESTS

- Teaching skills in Elementary Education K-8 with strong academic training in science and social studies
- Taught in diverse settings with at-risk and special needs students
- International student teaching experience and living with a host family
- Volunteer service experience in Armenia

EDUCATIONAL PREPARATION

The University of Iowa, Iowa City, B.A. degree May 1999 *with honors*
      Major: Elementary Education   Minors: Science and Social Studies
      Dean's List   President's List   Mortar Board

STUDENT TEACHING EXPERIENCE

Fifth/Sixth Grade, West Elementary, Omaha, Nebraska, 9/99 - 10/99
Year 7 (Sixth Grade) Kaiapoi School, Kaiapoi, New Zealand, 10/99 - 12/99
- Implemented a positive and proactive classroom management system
- Effectively used a variety of teaching strategies including cooperative learning and a hands-on/manipulative approach to math and science
- Guided students through checkpoint reading system and Writing Workshop
- Incorporated music, drama, sports, art, and applied technology
- Initiated service-learning program and assisted in organization of class field trips and syndicate outings
- Evaluated student behavior and academic performance in preparation for student and parent conferences

PRACTICA EXPERIENCE

Fifth Grade, service learning, Central Elementary, Spring 1997
Multiage Grouping, remedial reading, Hills Elementary, Fall 1996
Fifth/Sixth Grade, all subject areas, Shimek Elementary, Spring 1995

SCIENCE HONORS RESEARCH

The Connie Belin National Center for Gifted Education, Spring 1998
- Conducted research examining relationships between science scores, gender, attributions and attitudes toward school
- Studied implications for classroom teachers

ACTIVITIES AND AWARDS

Honors Opportunity Program	Foundation for International Education
Traveling Trunks Volunteer	Classroom Volunteer, Dyer Elementary
Iowa State Education Association	Ronald McDonald House Volunteer

OTHER

International:
Armenian Reading Project, International Student Volunteers, Summer 1998
- Developed programs with high school and college students
- Worked in community-based programs during breaks
New Zealand Student Teaching, Fall 1999
- Lived with a host family and participated in cultural events
- Traveled throughout New Zealand and visited several schools

REFERENCES

Available upon request. View my Web site at: www.erin.teach.htm

JILL HALSTED

Present Address:
International School of Brussels
19 Kattenberg
1170 Brussels, Belgium
(322) 555-67-27

Stateside Address:
221 College Street
Any City, State 12345
(101) 555-0009

CURRENT EMPLOYMENT

1998-present **Multiage Elementary Teacher,** ages 7-10
International School of Brussels, Brussels, Belgium
Team leader for science and math responsible for organizing block
schedules and team planning time. Teach science and mathematics
using hands-on activities, maniuplatives, and specialized technology
applications; create learning centers with emphasis on developing higher
order thinking strategies; team-teach social studies and language arts;
collaborate with teachers, support staff and administrators to create a
positive and supportive learning environment for students from over
35 countries speaking 20 languages.

PROFESSIONAL SERVICE

1998-present Building level respresentative, Brussels International Parent Consortium
Chair, Technology Committee and Resource Team for Elementary
Teachers
Member, Site-Based Team for Building Expenditures and Expansion
Chaperone, High School Humanities Field Trip to London, Paris, and
Athens

TEACHING EXPERIENCE

1990-1996 **Elementary Teacher,** in self-contained Grade 3 classroom.
Faulkton Elementary School, Faulkton, South Dakota

1988-1990 **Elementary Teacher**, Grade 4 (3 years), Grade 3 (5 years)
Loneman School Corporation, Oglala, South Dakota

EDUCATION

1998 Master's Degree in Elementary Education
University of South Dakota, Vermillion, South Dakota

1988 Bachelor's Degree in Education
Sinte Gleska College, Rosebud, South Dakota

RELEVANT INFORMATION

U. S. citizen; married, husband is secondary science teacher and coach; daughter, age 3
References available at Teacher Education Center, Any City, State 12345   (101) 555-0008

Katrina Kyarski

221 College Street
Any City, State 12345 USA
(101) 555-0009

OBJECTIVE

ESL Teacher in Japan

Personal attributes include honesty, courtesy, responsibility, punctuality, and fairness.

EDUCATION

College of William and Mary, Williamsburg, Virginia
B.A. Degree - June 1999   *graduated with distinction*
Double Major: English and Philosophy

COURSE HIGHLIGHTS

Modern English Grammar	Psychology of Teaching
American Writers	Philosophy East and West
Women in Literature	Ancient Philosophy Seminar

EXPERIENCE

Teaching Related:

English Tutor, Academic Support Center, College of William and Mary
September 1999 - May 2000

Temporary English Test Specialist, College Testing Program
Washington D.C. Fall semester 1998

Travel:

Extensive travel in Canada, Mexico, and United States
Participated in 1998 Black Hills summer archaeological dig
Semester exchange program with Université de Moncton, 1997

Language:

Native English speaker
Spanish, read, write and speak (5 semesters)
Japanese (2 semesters)

COLLEGE ACTIVITIES

Student Alumni Association
College Flute Choir
Delta Delta Delta (Chair, Community Service)
Student Volunteer, Hospice Road Races

References available upon request

JAMES DOLMAN

221 College Street, Any City, State 12345, (101) 555-0009 (home)
(101) 555-1111 (school)

OVERVIEW:

• Headmaster	10 years	• **Teacher**	5 years
• Adjunct Professor	5 years	• **International**	
• Principal	6 years	**Volunteer**	2 years

CURRENT EXPERIENCE:

Headmaster, The Antilles School, St. Thomas, Virgin Islands, 1989-present. Administrative responsibility for The Antilles School—an independent college preparatory day school offering instruction from early childhood to grade 12. Student body comprises 430 students from diverse racial, ethnic, and national origins. The 27-acre campus consists of five separate classroom buildings, two libraries, and numerous athletic fields.

Adjunct Professor, College of Education, University of Virgin Islands, St. Thomas 1994-present. Teaching responsibility for the on-site methods component of the Social Science Methods class. Students are introduced to lesson design, classroom management strategies, teaching styles, test construction, and evaluation methods.

PROFESSIONAL EXPERIENCES:

Principal, St. Margaret's School, San Juan Capistrano, California, 1986-1990
Principal/Lead Teacher, Libreville Day School, Libreville, Gabon, 1983-1985
K-12 Teacher, Libreville Boys' School, Libreville, Gabon, 1981-1983
Secondary Teacher, Aiken High School, Aiken, South Carolina, 1978-1981
Volunteer, Heifer Project International, Ghana, South America, 1976-1978

SPECIAL TRAINING & INSTITUTES:

Oxford University, Oxford, England, Summer 1998
> *Topic: Global Learning and Social Responsibility*
Teacher's College, Columbia University, New York, Summer 1996
> *Topic: Management by Consensus*
Princeton University, Princeton, New Jersey, Summer 1994
> *Topic: New School Concept*
University of Montana, Missoula, Montana, Summer 1992
> *Topic: Grant Writing for Private Schools*

ACADEMIC TRAINING:

Educational Specialist Degree	University of South Carolina, 1986
	Columbia, South Carolina
Bachelor of Arts Degree	Reed College, 1976
Social Science and Psychology	Portland, Oregon

PROFESSIONAL MEMBERSHIPS:

Middle States Association of Schools and Colleges
National Association of Independent Schools
Caribbean Counselors Association
National Association of Secondary School Principals
American Association for Counseling and Development

References provided upon request

STEPHANIE J. HANSEN

221 College Street   Any City, State 12345   (101) 555-0009

sjhansen@newark.edu

INTERESTS AND ATTRIBUTES

- Experienced secondary teacher with second-language acquitsition
- Skilled in numerous technology applications
- Commitment to teamwork and creating an optimum learning environment
- Enjoy working and living in new settings
- Flexible and adaptable; creative problem-solver

EDUCATIONAL BACKGROUND

English Education, Master of Arts, 1999, University of Delaware - Newark

English/History, Bachelor of Arts, 1996, Delaware State College - Dover

PROFESSIONAL EXPERIENCE:

- English Teacher, Newark High School, Newark, Delaware, 1996-present Current responsibilities include teaching general English, American Authors survey course (grades 11/12), and an advanced composition course (grade 12). Developed curriculum for composition course, designed and implemented learning centers for general English, and served on textbook selection committee for the authors course. Work closely with teachers in history and art to teach integrated units. Collaboration in planning, instruction, and assessment. Supervise college practicum and student teachers.

TRAVEL AND LANGUAGES

Co-Sponsor, Newark Area High Schools Tour of France, 1998

Toured Southern Europe and North Africa, Summer 1995

AFS Student, Orleans, France, Junior Year 1991

French - excellent reading and writing skills, good conversational ability

Spanish - reading knowledge

HONORS:

Graduated with highest honors, Delaware State College

Awarded the President's Young Scholar Certificate

PROFESSIONAL AFFILIATIONS:

Phi Delta Kappa	Delaware Education Association
Pi Lambda Theta	National Council of Teachers of English

RELEVANT DATA:

Interests: tennis, photography, classical music, antiques, traveling

Citizenship: U.S.A.; Single, no dependents

CREDENTIALS

Career Planning & Placement Office, Any City, State 12345 (101) 555-0008

LEE PHILLIPS

221 College Street, Any City, State 12345 (101) 555-0009
lee-phillips@ndu.edu   or   www.lee.irish.htm

STRENGTHS

- ▸ Adapt to new situations and surroundings quickly; inquisitive and self-motivated
- ▸ Conversational speaking ability in Spanish, comprehend French
- ▸ Public speaking skills, writing abilities, and organizational strengths
- ▸ Intensive training in communication skills; interested in working with all ages
- ▸ Work experience with youth in an urban environment

ACADEMIC BACKGROUND

Notre Dame University, Notre Dame, Indiana, B.A. Degree, *with honors*, May 2000
        Major: Communication Studies and Theater   Minor: English
Study Abroad, May 1999, The London Performing Arts Program

TEACHING EXPERIENCE

Mayor's Youth Employment Volunteer Program, South Bend, Summer 1999
        Responsibilities include planning, organizing, and implementing community
        service projects for urban youth who need to develop work skills and habits.
        Build trusting relationships with youth to help develop ways to enrich lives.
Volunteer Teaching Experience, North City High, Michigan City, Spring 1999
        Responsibilities included observing and assisting in a skills development
        classroom for 100 hours. Taught and assessed small reading groups.
Swimming and Sailing Lessons, 1995 - present
        Responsibilities included teaching basic techniques to toddlers through adults.
        Organized curriculum through Water Safety Instructor Certification.

VOLUNTEER EXPERIENCE

Crisis Center, South Bend, Indiana, 1999 - present. Intensive training to volunteer
        in crisis situations, suicide intervention, and making appropriate referrals.
Tutor for English as a Second Language students, University Speaking Lab, 1998.
        Taught Cambodian, Russian, and Laotian students English grammar.
Free Lunch Program, South Bend and Northern Counties, Inc., 1997-1998
        Collaborated with various community volunteers to prepare and serve food.

CAMPUS ACTIVITIES AND LEADERSHIP

Student Advisor and Recruitment Host, University Admissions Office, Notre Dame
University, 1998 - present. Work with potential students and their parents.
        Answer questions and concerns about campus and academic life.
Dance Marathon Coordinator, Notre Dame University Greek System, Fall 1997
        Organized fraternities and sororities to raise money for local pediatrics unit.

References available upon request.

21

A FINAL WORD ABOUT RESUMES

Skimming through even a few of the hundred and one résumés presented in this book should make it a bit easier for you to confront the task of writing your own. Of course, a résumé is vitally important if you are looking for employment, but even if you have no urgent or immediate need for it, the time you spend creating a résumé is time well spent.

Whether you are constructing your very first résumé or just updating one that has served you well in the past, take full advantage of the opportunity to record and describe your accumulated experiences and achievements. Your résumé is a professional record of real consequence. It is not just a factual statement of dates and places but an account of genuine significance that can chart progress toward goals, point to authentic abilities, suggest skills to update or strengthen, and even propose new avenues to explore. For this reason alone, any teacher can benefit from preparing a résumé and cultivating the habit of periodic updating and revision.

Although it is not a magic key, a good résumé can open doors that would otherwise remain closed to you. As a means of introduction, it can help you through the employment process, support your efforts to secure funding or grants for special projects, or highlight your particular strengths and skills for leadership roles or positions.

When the time comes to submit your résumé, you can revise, rearrange, and rework the information to make it directly relevant to your specific purpose. Revising and adapting are important processes, but they are only a means to an end. You could fiddle forever attempting to find the precise word, the ideal format, the most efficient, striking, pointed, or focused arrangement of categories, not to mention the most attractive layout, the most legible font, and the most appealing paper to convey your message. But eventually your résumé must stand alone. Except for absolute accuracy about dates and locations, and impeccable spelling and grammar, don't try to be perfect—and don't worry about final versions. As your career develops, your résumé will undergo many changes, many variations. Your goal is not to write the definitive résumé, just a positive, accurate, honest document that establishes and fosters your professional image.

BARRON'S POCKET GUIDES—

The handy, quick-reference tools that you can count on—no matter where you are!

A Pocket Guide
Synonyms

Quick help in finding different words with similar meanings. Includes list of 250 overused words. An aid to better writing style. Easy-to-use alphabetical format.

Arthur H. Bell, Ph.D.
Barron's Educational Series, Inc.

ISBN: 0-8120-4843-1
$7.95 Canada $10.50

BARRON'S
A POCKET GUIDE TO
Correct English
Third Edition

Sentence construction
Spelling
Punctuation
Usage
Essays and letter writing and more

Michael Temple

ISBN: 0-8120-9816-1
$6.95 Canada $8.95

BARRON'S
A POCKET GUIDE TO
Correct Grammar
Third Edition

Parts of speech
Correct usage
Review of common grammatical errors and how to correct them

V. Hopper, C. Gale, and R. Foote
Revised by Benjamin W. Griffith

ISBN: 0-8120-9815-3
$6.95 Canada $8.95

BARRON'S
A POCKET GUIDE TO
Correct Punctuation
Third Edition

Punctuation marks and how to use them
Emphasis on the logic of punctuation

Robert Brittain

ISBN: 0-8120-9814-5
$6.95 Canada $8.95

A Pocket Guide
Thesaurus

Quick help in finding alternate words with similar meanings and antonyms. Includes list of overused words. Easy-to-use alphabetical format.

Arthur H. Bell, Ph.D.
Barron's Educational Series, Inc.

ISBN: 0-8120-4845-8
$7.95 Canada $10.50

BARRON'S
A POCKET GUIDE TO
Correct Spelling
Third Edition

26,000 often-misspelled words
Arranged alphabetically and divided into syllables
Easy-to-remember spelling rules

Francis Griffith

ISBN: 0-8120-9813-7
$6.95 Canada $8.95

BARRON'S
A POCKET GUIDE TO
Vocabulary
Third Edition

More than 3,000 words that appear on SAT I and other standardized tests
Listed alphabetically with concise definitions and example sentences

Samuel Brownstein, Mitchel Weiner and Sharon Weiner Green

ISBN: 0-8120-9818-8
$6.95 Canada $8.95

BARRON'S
A POCKET GUIDE TO
Study Tips
Third Edition

Tips for scheduling and organizing study time
How to take useful notes
How to correct your weak points

W. H. Armstrong, M. W. Lampe and G. Ehrenhaft

ISBN: 0-8120-9812-9
$6.95 Canada $8.95

Barron's EDUCATIONAL SERIES, INC.
250 Wireless Boulevard • Hauppauge, New York 11788
In Canada: Georgetown Book Warehouse
34 Armstrong Avenue • Georgetown, Ontario L7G 4R9

Prices subject to change without notice. Books may be purchased at your bookstore, or by mail from Barron's. Enclose check or money order for total amount plus 15% for postage and handling (minimum charge $4.95). New York state residents add sales tax. All books are paperback editions.

(#18) R 11/97

BEGINNING SPANISH FOR TEACHERS OF HISPANIC STUDENTS

Pamela J. Sharpe, Ph.D.

Here at last is a valuable self-instruction program for primary and secondary school teachers who speak English only, but need some practical knowledge of Spanish so that they can work with Hispanic students. The boxed set consists of—

- A 280-page illustrated combination textbook and workbook
- 376 dialogue flashcards bound into a separate book of perforated card stock paper
- Four 90-minute cassettes
- A 92-page audioscript book

The program presents 24 lessons that start with greeting children in Spanish and introducing yourself, giving children basic instructions including taking out and putting away school supplies, participating in learning activities, praising children's good work, correcting their mistakes and behavior, questioning and comforting a child who is injured, participating in holiday celebrations and special events, communicating with Hispanic parents, and much more.

The main book's text and illustration are coordinated to match the dramatized conversations on cassette. It features many quizzes and exercises that will help you learn and retain the Spanish you need to know. The accompanying dialogue cards contain simple line drawings that depict a teacher and students engaged in a variety of classroom activities. Each card coincides with key words and phrases in the lessons and together will help you increase your memory retention.

Pamela J. Sharpe, Ph.D., is Associate Professor of English as a Second Language and Bilingual Education at Northern Arizona University in Yuma.

A quick, practical way to learn Spanish for use in a classroom setting.

ISBN 0-8120-8118-8

$35.00 Canada $45.95

Barron's Educational Series, Inc.
250 Wireless Blvd., Hauppauge, NY 11788
Order toll-free: 1-800-645-3476 • Order by fax: 1-516-434-3217
Canadian orders: 1-800-645-3476 • Fax in Canada: 1-800-887-1594

Visit us at www.barronseduc.com

Books and packages may be purchased at your local bookstore or by mail directly from Barron's. Enclose check or money order for total amount, plus sales tax where applicable and 15% for postage and handling (minimum $4.95). All books advertised here are paperback editions. Prices subject to change without notice.

#74 10/97